Writing Handbook

GRADE

4

Houghton Mifflin Harcourt

Contents

Contents

How to Use This Book

Writing is a great tool. It can help you solve problems as well as express yourself. For example, you can use it to nail down an idea or hammer out a point. This handbook will help you discover ways to use this tool well.

What Is a Handbook?

If writing is a tool, then this handbook is the how-to manual. It contains clear definitions, strategies, models, and key practice. Refer to its pages as much as you need to before, during, and after writing.

Sections of This Book

This handbook has three sections:

1. **Writing Forms**—Definitions, labels, and models of key writing forms
2. **Writing Strategies**—Ideas and methods that you can use for every kind of writing
3. **Writing Models and Forms**—Models of good writing

How to Find Information

Find information in this book in two different ways:

- **Use the contents page.** Find the section you need, and then turn to the entry that most closely matches the topic you want.
- **Use the tabs at the top of left-hand pages.** The names of the tabs change with each section. You can flip to sections that interest you to skim and scan for the information that you seek.

Purposes for Writing

When you write, one of the first things you should do is think about your purpose. Your **purpose** is your main reason for writing. There are many purposes for writing, but four of the main ones are to inform, to explain, to narrate, or to persuade.

● To Inform

To inform is to give or share information. This means writing and sharing facts and details. Some examples of writing that to inform include reports, informational essays, and instructions.

● To Explain

To explain means to tell more about a topic by telling what, why, and how. Some kinds of writing that explain are instructions, how-to paragraphs, and explanations.

● To Narrate

To narrate means to tell a story, whether that story is true or made up. Some examples of narrative writing include personal narratives, stories, and biographies. (Note: biographies also inform.)

● To Persuade

To persuade means to convince someone else to agree with your opinion or goal, or to take action. Examples of writing to persuade include opinion paragraphs, persuasive essays, and book and film reviews.

Understanding Task, Audience, and Purpose (TAP)

Knowing your purpose is one way to help you select the type of writing you might do. You also have to consider your **audience**, or for whom you are writing. For example, the words you use in writing to a friend are likely to be different than those you use with someone you have never met.

Knowing your purpose and your audience will help you quickly select your **task**, or writing form. For example, if you want to tell your teacher and classmates about a topic you have been studying, you might choose to share the information as a report, an essay, or a multimedia presentation.

Decide your task, audience, and purpose, or **TAP**, before you begin writing. Your task is what you are writing. Your purpose is why you are writing. Your audience is for whom you are writing. Your teacher may give you the TAP for an assignment. Sometimes you will decide on your own.

Ask yourself these questions.

Task: <u>What</u> am I writing?

Do I want to write a letter, a report, or something else?

Audience: For <u>whom</u> am I writing?

Am I writing for a teacher, a friend, myself, or someone else?

Purpose: <u>Why</u> am I writing?

Am I writing to persuade someone, to give information, or for another reasons?

The Writing Process

Writing is a lot like any other goal you set. Often, you need a plan to get started. Chances are also good that once you get going, you'll want to make changes to whatever you're doing to make it better.

The writing process is a five-stage strategy that was designed to help you write well. It helps you know how to get started. It also helps you think through what you're going to write and then change it and improve it along the way. The best part about the writing process is that you can return to any of the stages while you're writing.

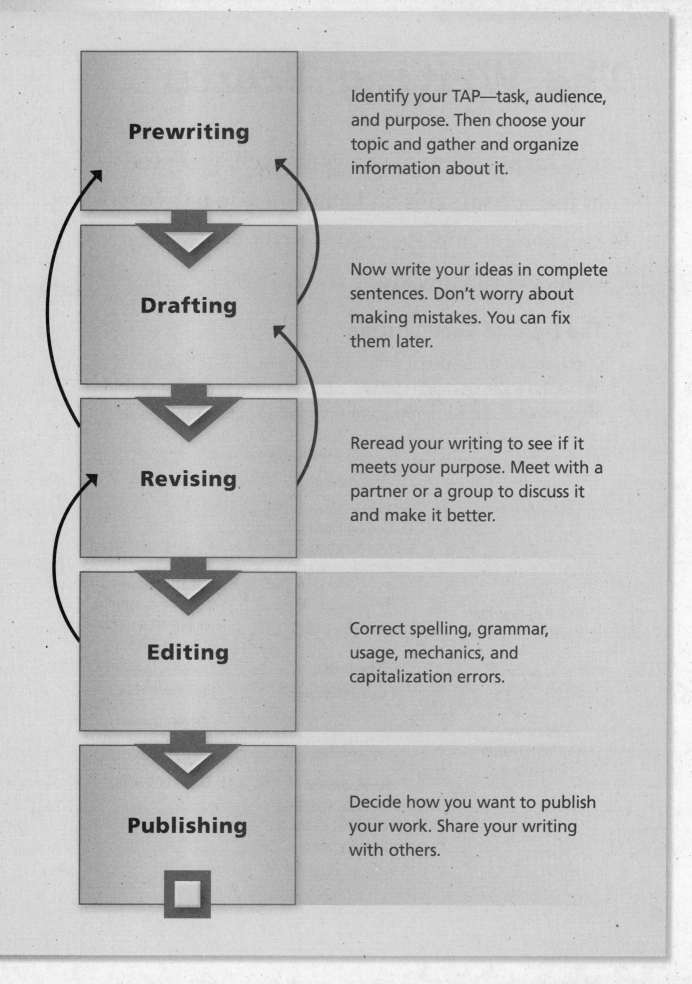

Prewriting

Identify your TAP—task, audience, and purpose. Then choose your topic and gather and organize information about it.

Drafting

Now write your ideas in complete sentences. Don't worry about making mistakes. You can fix them later.

Revising

Reread your writing to see if it meets your purpose. Meet with a partner or a group to discuss it and make it better.

Editing

Correct spelling, grammar, usage, mechanics, and capitalization errors.

Publishing

Decide how you want to publish your work. Share your writing with others.

The Writing Traits

You know that to play a game well, you need to use special skills and strategies. In baseball, for example, a player needs to hit well, catch well, and run quickly.

The Traits of Good Writing

Good writing takes special skills and strategies, too. This web shows the traits, or characteristics, of good writing. You will learn much more about each of these traits in other parts of this book.

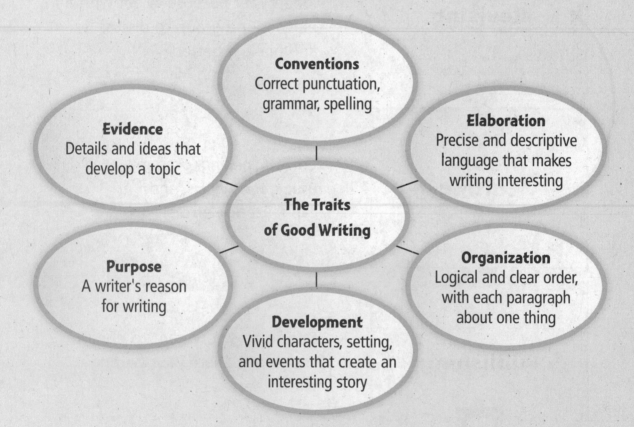

Conventions
Correct punctuation, grammar, spelling

Evidence
Details and ideas that develop a topic

Elaboration
Precise and descriptive language that makes writing interesting

The Traits of Good Writing

Purpose
A writer's reason for writing

Organization
Logical and clear order, with each paragraph about one thing

Development
Vivid characters, setting, and events that create an interesting story

Traits Checklist

As you practice writing, ask yourself these questions.

☑ **Evidence**	Do I explain ideas with details and examples? Do I support opinions with facts and details?
☑ **Organization**	Are my ideas in a clear order? Do I have a beginning, a middle, and an ending? Are my ideas grouped in paragraphs? Do I use transitions, such as time-order words?
☑ **Purpose**	Is my reason for writing clear?
☑ **Elaboration**	Do I use vivid and precise words and phrases to develop my topic or tell a story?
☑ **Development**	Did I include details that help readers visualize the characters and settings? Did I tell the story events in an interesting way?
☑ **Conventions**	Are my spelling, grammar, and punctuation correct?

Descriptive Paragraph

A **descriptive paragraph** describes, or tells about, a person, place, thing, or event using vivid details and sensory words.

Parts of a Descriptive Paragraph

- A topic sentence that clearly names the person, place, thing, or event to be described
- Sentences that use vivid details, active verbs, and colorful adjectives
- Sensory words that help readers see, hear, feel, smell, and taste what you are describing
- Position words that tell where things are
- An ending sentence that ties ideas together

Topic Sentence

Vivid Details

Sensory Words

Ending Sentence

To me, nothing beats a day at the seashore. One of my favorite things to do is build sand castles. I use the wet, slimy sand near the water for my castles. It holds together well. **In the distance**, there are some big, rolling waves. I like to dive into those waves and let them carry me to shore. The water is icy cold when I first jump in, and I taste its salt long after I get out. I hear seagulls call from **above** as they dive for fish. **On** the sand, I look for shells to add to my collection. Some feel smooth and some feel rough. **Next** to the water, the wet shells sparkle in the sunlight. The seashore is a beautiful place to visit!

Other Position Words
On the left
Past
Behind
In front of
Around the corner
Beside
Next to

Name _Olivia Klave_

Follow your teacher's directions to complete Frames 1 and 2.

We Do 1

My Beutiful room is one
of my favorite places. _It is one of my favorite place to_ _spend alone time_
In the distance, _I see my giant bed my brown_
desk, and my newly built bookcase. .

_____.Above

I see my spinning fan

_____.

Next to _____.

_____

You Do 2

_____

_____

_____. Next to _____

_____. Beside _____

_____.

On the left _____.

_____. As I

leave, I see _____.

You Do 3 On a separate sheet of paper, use your prewriting plan
to write a descriptive paragraph about an everyday
place you have visited recently, or plan and write a
new paragraph about a place you saw on a trip.

Story

A **story** tells about either a real or an imaginary experience or event. A true story tells about something that actually happened to the writer.

✏ Parts of a Story

- A catchy beginning that introduces the main characters and the time and place of the story
- Events that are told in time order, or sequence
- Vivid details and dialogue that help readers understand the characters, events, and setting
- An ending that tells how the story worked out

Beginning
Makes readers want to find out more

→ On Thursday, everyone in our class picked animals for a report except Jason, who was out sick that day.

"It's not fair," Jason complained, "because *I* want to find out about leopards. Sara took my topic."

Events
Tell what happened in time order

→ **During** lunch, I tried to help Jason. I named a few interesting animals. None wowed him. **After** lunch, we went outside for gym. I spotted an odd creature **as soon as** I ran to the field. It crawled along the warm, red bricks of the school building.

Strong Details and Dialogue
Include sights, sounds, and the words characters say

→ "Hey, Jason, here's your science report!" I shouted excitedly, pointing to a thin, brown twig.

"We're studying animals," Jason snapped.

"That walking stick *is* an insect," I explained.

Other Transitions
First
Next
Then
During
Meanwhile
Later
Last
Until

Ending
Wraps up the story and tells how the writer felt

→ Jason grinned. **Finally**, he had a subject he liked! I felt proud to help my friend.

Name _____

Follow your teacher's directions to complete the frame.

1   A problem that I helped a friend solve was _____

_____.

First, _____

_____. Then _____.

_____

_____. Next, _____

_____

_____

_____

_____

_____. Later, _____

_____

_____. After that, _____

_____

_____. Finally, _____

_____

I felt _____.

2   On a separate sheet of paper, write a true story about the funniest joke you ever played on someone.

3   On a separate sheet of paper, use your prewriting plan to write a true story, or make a new plan to write about a time when you stood up for something you believe in.

Dialogue

In a story, **dialogue** is the words characters say. Dialogue helps the reader imagine what the characters are like and how they act.

✏ Parts of a Dialogue

- Words that sound like real speech
- Words that fit a character's age and personality
- Actions and movements to show how a characters feel and act
- Correct punctuation to help readers understand who is speaking and how something is being said

In August, Mina and Grandma visited White Sands Beach. They waded in shallow water, scooping up pretty shells. Suddenly, Grandma froze.

Lifelike Words
Use words that sound natural and show what a character is like

"Hey, what's wrong?" **asked Mina.**

"Don't move," **Grandma hissed.** "There's a jellyfish right by your leg. It can sting!"

"Tell—tell me when it swims away," **Mina whispered** nervously, staring straight ahead.

Actions and Movements
Tell what characters do and how they move

Soon, the tide gently pushed the slimy jellyfish deeper into the sea. Grandma smiled at Mina.

Other Speaker's Tags
she shouted
he wondered
they laughed
I exclaimed
my sister cried
the teacher sighed
the man replied

"It's gone, honey."

Mina relaxed and raced out of the water onto the dry sand. She hugged her grandmother tightly.

Punctuation
Use quotation marks to set off a character's words

"Thanks for warning me," **Mina said** gratefully. "Next time, I'll look where I'm stepping when I go hunting for shells."

Name _____

Follow your teacher's directions to complete the frame.

We Do
1

_____ said, "_____

_____

_____."

_____ answered, "_____

_____

_____."

Then _____ asked, "_____

_____?"

"_____

_____

_____ ," replied _____

_____.

"_____

_____ !" exclaimed _____

"_____

_____ ," _____ said.

You Do
2 On a separate sheet of paper, write a dialogue
between two friends who are having an argument.

You Do
3 On a separate sheet of paper, use your prewriting
plan to write dialogue, or make a new plan to write a
dialogue between a coach and a player.

Fictional Narrative: Prewriting

A **fictional narrative** is a made-up story about characters who solve a problem.

Prewriting

- First, brainstorm characters, a setting, and a problem.
- Next, choose your topic. List what happens in the beginning, middle, and ending.
- Finally, use a graphic organizer to plan your writing.

Characters: two girls, (father and daughter) scout troop

Setting: a garage sale, (the mall) a cabin

Problem: break a vase, (want a kitten,) caught in a storm

Setting	Characters
Mall: animal shelter booth	Joan: eager, impatient Her father: careful, kind

Plot

Beginning

Joan and her dad are at a special booth set up by the animal shelter in the mall. She wants to adopt an orange kitten.

Middle

Dad says they must ask Mom first, but Joan is afraid that the kitten won't be there when they return.

Climax

Joan's mom and dad talk about whether Joan can have the kitten.

Ending

Joan's parents say yes. They go to the mall, and Joan is happy to find that the kitten is still there.

Name _____

Follow your teacher's directions to complete the activity.

Setting	Characters

Plot

Beginning

Middle

Climax

Ending

On a separate sheet of paper, fill in a graphic organizer like the one above. Write your ideas for a fictional narrative about a character who loses something important.

On a separate sheet of paper, prewrite a fictional narrative. You can also use what you have learned to improve an old plan.

Fictional Narrative

A **fictional narrative** tells about made-up characters who solve a problem.

Parts of a Fictional Narrative

- A beginning that introduces characters and a problem
- Descriptions that include active and colorful words
- A middle that shows how characters deal with the problem
- A climax that tells the most exciting part of the story
- An ending that tells how characters solve the problem

Beginning
Introduces the characters and problem

Descriptions
Include active and colorful words

Middle
Shows how characters deal with problem

Climax
The most exciting part of the story

Ending
Tells how the problem was solved

"Please, Dad!" Joan pleaded. The town animal shelter had set up a special booth at the mall. Joan really wanted the tiny orange kitten she was holding.

"We must talk to your mother first," her father said.

"But I don't want to leave it!" Joan whined.

Her father asked if the shelter would hold the kitten for a day. That wasn't possible, the worker explained. Disappointed, Joan pouted all the way home.

That night, Joan's mother told her that kittens take lots of work. Joan would have to brush it, feed it, and clean up after it every day. Joan eagerly agreed to it all, and her parents finally said yes.

The next day, the family went back to the mall. Joan raced inside. The kitten was there, looking right at Joan. They were already becoming friends!

Other Transitions
At first
Earlier
Yesterday
Last week, month, year
After that
Then
Finally

Name _____

Follow your teacher's directions to complete the frame.

We Do 1 "Please, Mom!" _____

_____.

_____

_____

_____. That night, _____

_____.

The next day, _____

_____

Later, _____

_____

_____. Then _____

_____

_____. After that, _____

_____

_____

You Do 2 On a separate sheet of paper, write a fictional narrative about a character who loses something important.

You Do 3 On a separate sheet of paper, use your prewriting plan to write a fictional narrative, or plan and write a new fictional narrative about a character who has a disagreement with his or her best friend.

News Report

A **news report** tells about a real event that happened recently.

Parts of a News Report

- A headline, or title, that uses strong words to catch the reader's attention
- A lead, or beginning paragraph, that introduces the most important information in an interesting way
- A body that gives true information about the event and answers the questions *who, what, when, where, why,* and *how*
- A quotation from a participant or an onlooker, if possible

Headline
Catches reader's attention →

Interesting Lead →

Body
Gives information about the event →

Quotation
Actual words of people who saw the event →

St. Petersburg Student Wins Science Award

By Marsha Sanders, March 12, 2013

Tampa—Wesley Jackson, a fourth-grader from St. Petersburg, won the Curie Science Award. His entry was a simple robot that picks up and moves books and other objects.

The award is given every year to one student who participates in the Statewide School Science Fair. Jackson was one of 54 students to enter the contest.

"We were excited by his work," said Thomas Garrett, a teacher who judged at the fair.

"I am happy all my hard work paid off," said Jackson. He plans to use the prize money to build another robot.

5 Ws + H
Who
What
When
Where
Why
How

Name _____

Follow your teacher's directions to complete the frame.

1

Local School Goes Green, Wins Big

The governor of Florida gave a prize to Jefferson Elementary School in Gainsville for being friendly to the environment.

_____

_____

_____

_____

One student said, "_____

_____."

_____

_____

_____

_____

_____

_____

2 On a separate sheet of paper, plan and write a news report about a school play or sporting event you attended.

3 On a separate sheet of paper, plan and write a news report about an event that took place in your town.

Informational Paragraph

An **informational paragraph** explains a subject, gives directions, or tells a reader how to do something. It includes facts, examples, definitions, and other details.

✏ Parts of an Informational Paragraph

- A topic sentence that introduces the main idea
- Supporting details that develop the main idea
- Use of precise words
- An ending that sums up the main idea

Topic sentence
Introduces the main idea

Supporting Details
Give facts, examples, and other information

Precise Words
Use words and phrases that clearly convey ideas

Ending
Sums up the main idea

   Playing with hoops is a very old custom. Long ago, children in Europe, the Americas, Africa, and Asia played with hoops. **For example**, by about 1,000 B.C., children in Egypt rolled large hoops made of dried vines. Later, ancient Greeks rolled metal hoops with a short stick. They decorated their hoops with bells. Ancient Romans and Native Americans used a hoop as a target. They threw spears through it as it rolled. In other cultures, children had hoop races. Teams sometimes played hoop battles. Players who knocked down the most hoops would win. **Also**, children played entertaining games of skill. They made gates by setting two bricks or stones a few inches apart. Then they tried to get their hoops through the narrow gates without touching the sides. Games like these have made playing with hoops popular around the world for thousands of years.

Other Transitions
In addition
Furthermore
As well
Such as
Besides
Likewise
Another
Moreover
However

Name _____

Follow your teacher's directions to complete the frame.

1 _____.

_____

For instance, _____

_____.

_____

_____.

_____

_____.

_____

_____ such as _____

_____

_____. In addition, _____

_____

_____. Also, _____

_____.

2 On a separate sheet of paper, write an informational paragraph about your favorite kind of food.

3 On a separate sheet of paper, use your prewriting plan to write an informational paragraph, or make a new plan to write about a famous monument.

Book Report

A **book report** is a summary of what a book is about, where it takes place, and what happens. It helps readers understand what a particular book is about.

Parts of a Book Report

- An introduction that clearly states the main idea
- A body that tells about the most important parts of the book
- A conclusion that sums up the book

Introduction
States the title, the author, and the kind of book

Charlie's Paintbrush is a fictional story by Beth Cody. The book is about a talented artist named Lily. Lily's dream is to go to art school.

Body
Tells about main characters, setting, and events

Every day, Lily takes the train to Brooklyn, New York. She paints in a tiny studio. One afternoon, a stray cat with a puffy tail visits her. Lily names the cat Charlie. **After** Charlie's fourth visit, Lily finds a long purple streak across the middle of her new painting. **Next**, she finds red paint smeared along the bottom. Who ruined her painting? She has no idea, so she sets a trap to find out. **Finally**, Lily realizes that Charlie thinks he is an artist, too.

Conclusion
Restates the title and author of the book

Later, Lily enters her new painting in an art contest. The judge likes the bold way she uses a paintbrush. Lily—and Charlie—win first prize. Read *Charlie's Paintbrush* by Beth Cody yourself to find out what Lily does with the prize money!

Other Transitions
First
Now
After that
During
After a while
Meanwhile
Then
Last

Name _____

Follow your teacher's directions to complete the frame.

1 _____.

_____. At first,

_____

_____. Then _____

_____

_____

_____. Next, _____

_____

_____

_____

_____

_____

_____. After that, _____

_____

_____. Finally, _____

_____

_____

2 On a separate sheet of paper, write a book report about a fictional book you have recently read.

3 On a separate sheet of paper, use your prewriting plan to write a book report, or make a new plan to write one about a book that tells about a real person in history.

Explanatory Essay: Prewriting

An **explanatory essay** tells what something is or why or how something happens. It informs readers about a topic.

Prewriting

- First, brainstorm a list of topics that you would like to explain. Select one topic.
- Gather facts and details about your topic. Look for precise words that will make your explanation clear.
- Use a graphic organizer like the idea-support map below to plan your essay.

Topic: Children's Day in Japan

Main idea: Children's Day is a holiday in Japan.

Facts and examples: Celebrated on May 5

Became national holiday in 1948

Celebrates health and happiness of children

Main idea: Japanese families decorate their homes for Children's Day.

Facts and examples: Display warrior dolls

Fly carp streamers

They hang irises or sprinkle baths with iris leaves

Main idea: People eat special foods for Children's Day.

Facts and examples: Rice cakes wrapped in bamboo

Bean-filled rice cakes wrapped in oak leaves

Name _____

Follow your teacher's directions to complete the activity.

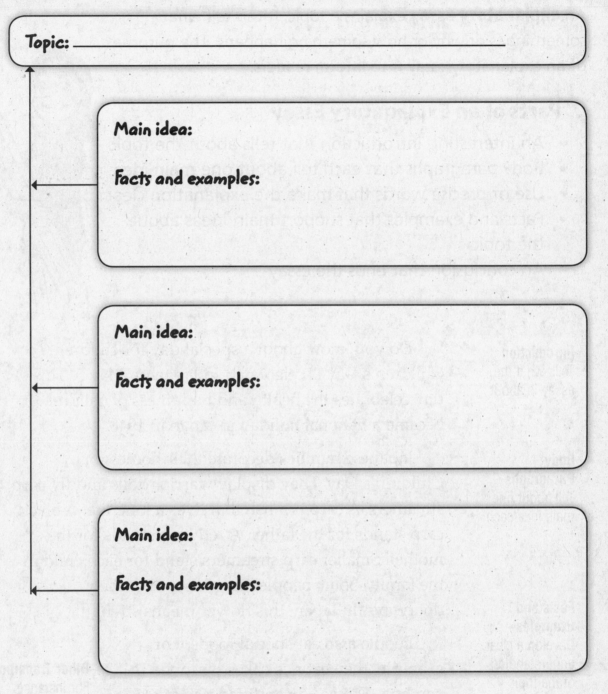

Explanatory Essay

An **explanatory essay** explains a topic. It can tell what something is or why or how something happens. The purpose of an explanatory essay is to inform readers.

Parts of an Explanatory Essay

- An interesting introduction that tells about the topic
- Body paragraphs that each tell about one main idea
- Use of precise words that make the explanation clear
- Facts and examples that support main ideas about the topic
- An conclusion that ends the essay

Introduction
Tells what the essay is about

→ Do you know about a special day for children? Children's Day is celebrated in Japan on May 5. This day celebrates the health and happiness of children. It became a national holiday in Japan in 1948.

Body Paragraphs
Tell about one main idea each

→ Japanese families decorate their homes for Children's Day. They display warrior dolls and fly carp streamers. A carp is a fish that lives a long life. A black carp stands for the father. A red carp stands for the mother. Smaller carp streamers stand for each child in the family. Some people hang irises over their doorways. In Japan, this flower means strength.

Facts and Examples
Develop a clear understanding of the topic

→ People **also** eat special foods. **For example**, they eat rice cakes wrapped in bamboo. They eat bean-filled rice cakes wrapped in oak leaves.

Other Transitions
For instance
Another
In order to
In other words
In particular
Additionally
Namely
As well

Conclusion
Draws the essay to a close

→ There are other Children's Day customs, **too**. But whatever traditions people follow, they show their wishes for strong, successful children.

Name _____

Follow your teacher's directions to complete the frame.

1 _____

_____.

_____. In addition, _____

_____.

_____

_____

_____. For example, _____

_____.

_____

_____ also _____

_____

_____

_____ as well. _____

_____

_____

_____.

2 On a separate sheet of paper, write an explanatory essay about a holiday you enjoy.

3 On a separate sheet of paper, use your prewriting plan to write an explanatory essay, or make a new plan to explain what something is or tell how or why something happens.

Persuasive Paragraph

A **persuasive paragraph** tries to convince readers to act or think in a certain way. It tells the writer's belief about a topic or an issue.

✏ Parts of a Persuasive Paragraph

- A topic sentence that states the writer's opinion
- Facts, reasons, and examples that support the writer's opinion
- Reasons that are organized in order of importance
- Persuasive words and phrases to convince the reader

Topic Sentence
Tell how you feel about a subject

Supporting Details
Include strong facts, reasons, and examples

Organization
List the most important reason first or last

Persuasive Language
Use words like *popular* or *wonderful* to convince the reader

A rabbit makes a good pet. **First of all**, rabbits are clean. They spend a lot of time grooming their fur, and they can be trained to use a litter box like cats do. **Second**, rabbits are playful. They play with toys just as dogs and cats do, and they will run or hop around the house for exercise. **Third**, rabbits make only a little noise. Unlike dogs, rabbits don't bark. They only quietly grunt or stamp their feet when they are angry or upset. **Also**, rabbits like to be with people. To show their affection, they will lick or nibble you. **Most of all**, rabbits are intelligent and can be trained to do tricks, obey simple commands, and come when you call them. Pet rabbits have become more popular than ever. In 2007, there were more than 6 million pet rabbits in the United States. Are you thinking of getting a pet? Having a pet rabbit is a wonderful experience.

Other Transitions
Above all
Next
Last
Most importantly
Mainly
In addition
Most significant
Least important

Name _____

Follow your teacher's directions to complete the frame.

We Do 1   I believe that _____

_____.

First, _____

_____

_____

_____. Second, _____

_____

Third, _____

_____

_____

_____. In addition, _____

_____

_____

_____. Most importantly, _____

_____

_____

You Do 2   On a separate sheet of paper, write a persuasive paragraph about an issue in your community that is important to you.

You Do 3   On a separate sheet of paper, use your prewriting plan to write a persuasive paragraph, or make a new plan to write about a change you believe must take place in your school.

Problem-Solution Composition

A **problem-solution composition** presents a problem and tells ways to solve it.

✏ Parts of a Problem-Solution Composition

- An introduction that presents the problem
- A body that offers possible reasons and examples
- Language to persuade your audience
- A conclusion that tells the best solution

Introduction
Presents the problem

→ We students do not have time to eat lunch, even though we get a whole hour. It should be enough time, but it never is! The lunch lines are so long that they often take thirty minutes to get through! Then we have to gulp down our food and race back to class. Something has to change!

Solutions
Suggest ideas for fixing the problem

→ **One way** to improve things might be to stagger lunch. First, one class would go. Then, fifteen minutes later, the next class would follow, and so on. The lines would be shorter, and we

Reasons and Examples
Tell how the solutions work

→ would spend more time eating and less time waiting. **A second** way would be to hire another cashier and add another line. With two checkout lines, we could sit down to eat a lot faster.

Other Transitions
Next
Because
As a result
Finally
In addition
For instance
In order to

Conclusion
Names the best solution and gives reasons why it is best

→ Clearly, **the best solution** would be to stagger lunch. No more workers would be needed, and there would not be a need to buy another cash register. The school would just stagger the schedule. That way, we would make the most of our lunch time!

Name _____

Follow your teacher's directions to complete the frame .

1 One problem we have at school is _____

_____.

_____

_____. One way _____

_____ . _____

_____

_____

_____. A second way _____

_____.

_____

_____

The best solution _____

_____

_____

_____.

2 On a separate sheet of paper, plan and write a problem-solution composition about a problem with your school's library, music room, or gym. Suggest at least one possible solution.

3 On a separate sheet of paper, use your prewriting plan to write a problem-solution composition, or plan and write a composition about a problem in your community.

Persuasive Letter

A **persuasive letter** is a letter that is written to convince the reader to do something specific.

Parts of a Persuasive Letter

- A beginning that states the purpose for the letter
- Facts, reasons, and examples that support the main points of the letter
- A friendly, sincere tone
- The six parts of a letter: sender's address, date, recipient's address, body, closing, and signature

110 Fair Street
Brooksville, FL 34601
December 15, 2012

Mayor Jackson Murphy
206 Front Street
Brooksville, FL 34601

Dear Mayor Murphy,

Beginning
Asks the reader to do something

Building Brooksville Skate Park was a great idea. **However**, the park is now in bad shape, and the town must fix it. **For example**, the main gate sags. **Also**, a few of the ramps have rusty nails sticking out. **In addition**, storms caused large cracks in the concrete bowl.

Details
Give specific facts, reasons, and examples

As a regular skateboarder, I feel the park is dangerous. Skaters can lose control and fall off their boards. **For this reason**, I hope

Tone
Sounds honest and positive

you'll briefly close the park for repairs and help make us kids safer.

Sincerely,

Matt Lucci

Other Transitions
Because
On the other hand
Nevertheless
For instance
In order to
Although
In fact
Therefore

Name _____

Follow your teacher's directions to complete the frame.

We Do
1

_____

_____

_____

_____

_____

_____

Dear _____,

_____ because _____

_____.

For instance, _____

_____. Also, _____

_____. Finally, _____

_____.

For this reason, _____

_____.

Sincerely,

_____

You Do
2 On a separate sheet of paper, write a persuasive letter to the editor of your local newspaper. It should be about a situation that you feel strongly about.

You Do
3 On a separate sheet of paper, use your prewriting plan to write a persuasive letter, or make a new plan to write a persuasive letter in which you make a specific request.

Persuasive Essay: Prewriting

In a **persuasive essay,** the writer tries to convince readers to take action or to think a certain way.

Prewriting

- First, brainstorm a list of topics that are important to you. Choose one that you have a strong opinion about.
- Then take notes about your topic. Look for reasons, facts, and examples that support your opinion.
- Use a graphic organizer to plan your persuasive essay.

Goal: <u>Our school needs a worm farm.</u>

Reason: It would help reduce garbage.

Facts and examples:
Two pounds of worms can eat a whole pound of fruits and vegetables and other waste. There would be less garbage for the school to send to the landfill.

Reason: Worms make compost.

Facts and examples:
Compost is natural food for plants. We could sell extra compost to make money for school projects.

Name _____

Follow your teacher's directions to complete the activity.

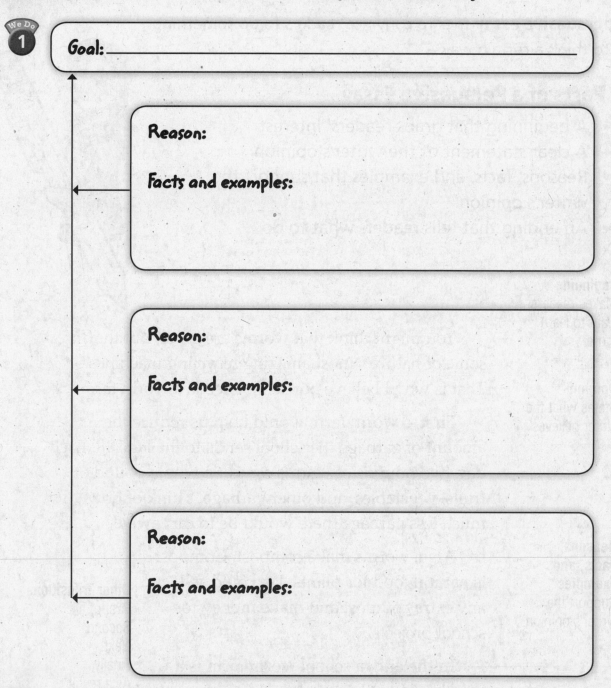

1 Goal: _____

Reason:

Facts and examples:

Reason:

Facts and examples:

Reason:

Facts and examples:

2 On a separate sheet of paper, fill in a graphic organizer like the one above. Write your opinion. Then list reasons, facts, and examples that support it.

3 On a separate sheet of paper, prewrite a persuasive essay. You can also use what you have learned to improve an old plan.

Persuasive Essay

A **persuasive essay** tries to convince readers to do something or to think a certain way.

Parts of a Persuasive Essay

- A beginning that grabs readers' interest
- A clear statement of the writer's opinion
- Reasons, facts, and examples that support the writer's opinion
- An ending that tells readers what to do

Beginning
Makes readers want to learn more

Opinion
States what the writer believes

   You might think that worms are gross, but they are some of nature's most amazing recycling machines. That is why I believe our school needs a worm farm.

   First, a worm farm would help us reduce the amount of garbage the school sends to the landfill. Each day, two pounds of worms can eat a whole pound of fruits, vegetables, and other garbage. Think of how much less garbage there would be to cart away!

Reasons, Facts, and Examples
Support the writer's opinion

   Also, worms make compost. Compost is natural food for plants. We could sell any extra compost and make money for school projects.

   In the end, a school worm farm is a winning idea. Come to the meeting Monday to vote YES for the worm farm.

Ending
Tells readers what to do

Other Transitions
First of all
Second
Next
Finally
As a result
In addition

Name _____

Follow your teacher's directions to complete the frame.

1 To help the environment, our school _____

_____

_____

First, _____

_____

_____

_____

_____

Also, _____

_____

_____

_____

_____

In the end, _____

_____

2 On a separate sheet of paper, write a persuasive essay about something the people in your town should do.

3 On a separate sheet of paper, use your prewriting plan to write a persuasive essay, or plan and write a new persuasive essay about something that is important to you.

Descriptive Paragraph

A **descriptive paragraph** describes, or tells about, a person, place, thing, or event. A descriptive paragraph helps create a picture in the reader's mind.

Parts of a Descriptive Paragraph

- A topic sentence that tells the subject of the paragraph
- Vivid details that clearly describe a person, place, thing, or event
- Strong words that help readers picture what is being described
- An ending that wraps up the description

Topic Sentence
Tells what the paragraph is about

Sensory Details
Tell how the subject looks, feels, sounds, smells, or tastes

Exact Words
Include specific nouns, verbs, and adjectives

Ending
Sums up the paragraph

Bailey Park is a great place to visit! A snack bar **next to** the parking lot sells yummy ice cream, cold drinks, popcorn, and other food. **Near** the entrance, noisy children play on slippery metal slides, climbing ladders, and blue plastic swings. Older kids race around the grassy soccer fields **behind** the swings. They also use the lighted basketball and tennis courts. There is a small picnic area **in the middle** of the park. You can eat your lunch **under** towering pine trees. Long green pine needles on the ground **by** the picnic tables feel as soft as a rug. Dad and I like to take the hiking trail **around** the marsh. It's a winding dirt path, which is marked with bright yellow triangles so you don't get lost. Sometimes, I hear frogs croaking in the reeds. Dad looks for interesting birds with his field glasses. Bailey Park has something for people of all ages.

Other Transitions
Above
Across
Below
Beside
Inside
Outside
At the bottom
Beyond

Name _____

Follow your teacher's directions to complete the frame.

We Do 1 A place I know well is _____

_____ .

Near _____

_____ .

Next to _____

_____

_____ . Behind _____

_____ .

Under _____

_____ .

_____

_____ in the middle of _____

_____

_____

_____ . Above _____

_____ _____

_____

You Do 2 On a separate sheet of paper, write a descriptive paragraph about a person you know well.

You Do 3 On a separate sheet of paper, use your prewriting plan to write a descriptive paragraph, or make a new plan to write about a familiar object in your room at home.

Friendly Letter

A **friendly letter** is written to someone the writer knows well. It includes informal, familiar language.

Parts of a Friendly Letter

- The writer's address and the date
- A greeting to the person who will receive the letter
- A body that makes up the main part of the letter
- Interesting details about the topic
- An informal, friendly voice
- A closing and the writer's signature

Greeting
Tells whom the letter is to

Body
The main part of the letter

Friendly Voice
Sounds like the person speaking

Interesting Details
Keep the reader interested

Closing and Signature

27 Palmetto Road
St. Petersburg, FL 33784
March 12, 2013

Dear Aunt Camille,

    Did Mom tell you the big news? I landed the lead part in the class play! When I first saw flyers for it, I knew I wanted to try out. I was so scared during the tryout! There was a bunch of other girls who wanted a part, too. First, we had to stand up in front of our classmates and read a few lines. We also took turns singing. The next day, my teacher announced that I had the part! I was so excited. I like being an actor. Will you come for the play? I'd love to see you!

Your niece,
Jenny

Closings
Your friend
Sincerely
Best wishes
Love

Name _____

Follow your teacher's directions to complete the frame.

We Do 1

_____

_____

_____

Dear _____,

    Did you hear the news? I won my soccer game last weekend! _____

_____

_____

_____

_____

_____

_____

_____

                    Sincerely,

_____

You Do 2 On a separate sheet of paper, plan and write a friendly letter to a friend or family member about something unusual that happened at school.

You Do 3 On a separate sheet of paper, use your prewriting plan to write a friendly letter, or plan and write a letter to a friend about something fun you did with your family.

Story

A **story** describes either a real or an imaginary experience or event. A fictional story is imagined or made up by the writer.

Parts of a Story

- A beginning that grabs the reader's attention
- Events told in time order, or sequence
- Use of synonyms, or words with the same or nearly the same meanings, to keep the story interesting
- An ending that tells how the story worked out

Beginning
Starts with an interesting opening

Events
Tell what happened in time order

Synonyms
Keep the story from using the same words too often

Ending
Wraps up the story

Thunk. Juan dropped the heavy microphone, which made a screeching noise as it smashed on the floor. **Then** he waited awkwardly for the music to start, but the dark auditorium was silent. Juan coughed and stared at the ceiling. **After** a few long minutes, the judges instructed Juan to go ahead—without music.

At last, Juan tried to sing, but his throat had tightened up because he was nervous. He sounded hoarse, like he had a bad cold. **When** Juan finished, he stomped off the stage and glared at the other singers. He had blown any chance to win.

Lisa felt awful about Juan's disaster and told him about her worst flop. "Meltdowns happen, but you'll learn how to deal with them. Do you want to rehearse together for the contest next month?" she asked.

Juan and Lisa practiced every day **until** the next competition. In the end, they won first prize.

Other Transitions
First
Next
After that
During
After a while
Meanwhile
Later
Last

Follow your teacher's directions to complete the frame.

1 _____

_____

At first, _____

_____. Then _____

_____

_____

_____. Next, _____

_____

_____

_____

_____

_____. After that, _____

_____

_____. Finally, _____

_____

_____

2 On a separate sheet of paper, write a story about someone who makes a new a friend.

3 On a separate sheet of paper, use your prewriting plan to write a story, or make a new plan to write about a person who wins something.

Personal Narrative: Prewriting

A **personal narrative** tells about something that happened to the writer and describes how the writer feels about the events.

Prewriting for Personal Narrative

- Brainstorm a list of true stories that happened to you.
- Pick one story that made a strong impression on you.
- Use a graphic organizer to plan your writing.

Topic Ideas

Giving food to a food bank

Making a hummingbird feeder

Riding a horse at Windy Farm

Event: My class wanted to give food to a food bank.

Details: My uncle is a chef. He offered to give us cooking lessons at his restaurant.

Event: Class met at my uncle's restaurant.

Details: We unpacked our cooking tools. My uncle showed us how to make different dishes. My group made pumpkin pie.

Event: We took the food to the food bank.

Details: Ms. Chao, the head of the food bank, thanked us. She said it would be the best Thanksgiving food a lot of people had. Everyone clapped for us. I felt great.

Follow your teacher's directions to complete the activity.

1

Event:

Details:

Event:

Details:

Event:

Details:

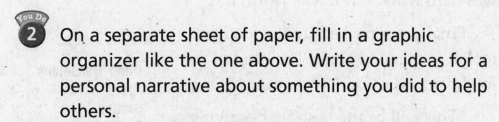

2 On a separate sheet of paper, fill in a graphic organizer like the one above. Write your ideas for a personal narrative about something you did to help others.

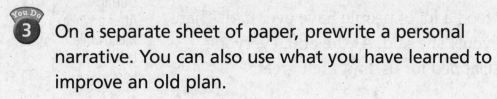

3 On a separate sheet of paper, prewrite a personal narrative. You can also use what you have learned to improve an old plan.

Personal Narrative

A **personal narrative** is a true story about something that happened to the writer. It tells how the writer feels about the events.

✏ Parts of a Personal Narrative

- A beginning that grabs readers' interest
- Events that really happened to the writer, told in time order
- Interesting details about the events
- The writer's feelings about what happened

Beginning
Makes readers want to find out more

> Have you ever wanted to be a chef? Everyone in my class got to be one this year. We wanted to donate food to a food bank. My uncle is a chef, and he offered to give us cooking lessons at his restaurant.

Events
Tell what happened in time order

> **To start**, the class met at the restaurant and unpacked our tools. **Then** my uncle showed us how to make different dishes. My group made pumpkin pie. It was hard work, but it was worth it!

Interesting Details
Include sights, sounds, and feelings

> **Finally,** we packed up the food and took it to the food bank. The head of the food bank, Ms. Chao, was waiting for us.

Ending
Tells how the writer felt

> "This will be the best Thanksgiving food a lot of people have ever had! Thank you!" she said. **At the end**, everyone clapped for us, and I felt great.

Other Transitions
First
Second
During
After a while
Meanwhile
Later
Last

Name _____

Follow your teacher's directions to complete the frame.

We Do 1

I had an amazing time when our class went _____

_____.

To start, _____

_____

_____. Then _____

_____

_____

_____

_____

_____

_____. Later, _____

_____

_____

_____. Last, _____

_____.

You Do 2

On a separate sheet of paper, write a personal narrative about one of the best things you ever did with your class.

You Do 3

On a separate sheet of paper, use your prewriting plan to write a personal narrative, or plan and write a new personal narrative about something you or your class did that helped other people.

Summary

A **summary** is a short retelling of a story, an article, or another piece of writing. It includes only the most important details about characters and events.

Parts of a Story Summary

- A topic sentence that tells what the summary is about
- The most important details of the story told in the writer's own words
- Events told in the order they happened

Topic Sentence
Tells what the summary is about

Important Details
Tell the most important parts of the story in the writer's own words

Events
Tell what happened in the same order as the story

The story "Riding Freedom" is about a girl named Charlotte who wants to drive stagecoaches. She practices until she is sure she can do it. The problem is that her friends James and Frank don't want her to drive. However, they say she can if she passes a test.

On the day of the test, there is a horrible storm, but Charlotte keeps the coach steady on the muddy road. **When** she gets to a wooden bridge, she has to make sure it is safe. She helps all her passengers walk across. **Then** she drives the coach toward the other side. Halfway there, the bridge starts to break. She hurries the horses along. Just as they get to the other side, the bridge falls down. All the passengers say Charlotte saved their lives. **In the end**, she knows she can have the job for sure.

Other Transitions
At first
Next
After that
Before
Later
Last
Finally
Eventually

Name _____

Follow your teacher's directions to complete the frame.

1 The story _____ is about

_____

_____.

The problem is _____

_____

_____. When _____

_____

_____

_____

Then _____

_____

_____

_____.

In the end _____

_____

_____

_____

2 On a separate sheet of paper, plan and write a summary of a book you read in class this year.

3 On a separate sheet of paper, use your prewriting plan to write a summary, or plan and write a summary of a favorite book.

Explanation

An **explanation** is writing that explains, or tells why or how something happens. The purpose of an explanation is to give readers information about a topic.

Parts of an Explanation

- A beginning that introduces the topic
- Information that is organized in a way that makes sense
- Facts and examples that support the topic
- An ending that sums up the main points

Beginning
Tells what the explanation is about

Organization
Presents information in a way that makes sense

Facts and Examples
Include details that help develop the explanation

Ending
Draws the explanation to a close

> Rainbow Bridge in southern Utah was formed millions of years ago. Rain and melted snow ran down Navajo Mountain. **When** the water flowed off the mountain, it created Bridge Creek. As the creek flowed toward the Colorado River, it passed through a canyon. For centuries, the creek washed over layers of rock in the canyon. The rushing water slowly wore away the rock **so that** it created thin rock walls. Eventually, the water broke through the thin walls and made a hole. **As a result**, a colorful stone bridge was carved out of the rock. The bottom of the bridge is reddish brown. The top is pink with dark red streaks. These rich colors come from iron and other minerals. Today, Rainbow Bridge arches high above Bridge Creek. It stretches more than 200 feet from one side to the other. Rainbow Bridge is one of the world's natural wonders!

Other Transitions
Because
Thus
Therefore
Consequently
In order to
Since
Accordingly
For this reason

Name _____

Follow your teacher's directions to complete the frame.

1 _____

_____

_____ because _____

_____

_____ . Since _____

_____

_____ . Therefore, _____

_____

_____ . _____

_____ so that _____

_____

For this reason, _____

_____

_____ . As a result _____

_____

2 On a separate sheet of paper, write an explanation about an important event in the history of your community or state.

3 On a separate sheet of paper, use your prewriting plan to write an explanation, or make a new plan to write about what causes a certain weather event, such as clouds or a rainbow.

Procedural Composition

A **procedural composition** tells how to do something. It presents step-by-step directions for how to complete a process.

Parts of a Procedural Composition

- A topic sentence that tells what readers will learn
- Steps in the process that are arranged in sequential order
- Transitions that make the order clear
- A conclusion, or ending, that tells the outcome of the process

Topic Sentence
Names the process

Steps
Tells what to do in sequence

Transitions
Make the order clear

Conclusion
Tells what results from following the steps

You can show the beauty of fall by drying colorful leaves for art projects. **First**, find leaves on the ground. Maple leaves are very pretty and great to use. **Before** you bring the leaves inside, shake off any water or bugs. **Next**, press the leaves between two paper towels to get rid of any water. **After that**, put each leaf between two sheets of paper. **Then** put your leaf-and-paper sandwich inside a thick, heavy book. Close the book and stack another big book on top. **After about two weeks**, your leaves should **finally** be dry. Your dried leaves can make colorful bookmarks. You can also paste leaves onto colored paper to make art to decorate your walls. You can even string them together to make yourself a beautiful chain of leaves to wear around your neck or wrist!

Other Transitions
Meanwhile
Later
Last
Second
Third

Name _____

Follow your teacher's directions to complete the frame.

1 Preparing for a big test takes time, energy, and concentration.

First, _____.

_____. Next, _____

_____

_____

_____

Then _____

_____

_____

_____

_____. After that, _____

_____

_____

_____

Finally, _____.

2 On a separate sheet of paper, plan and write a procedural composition about how to make your favorite craft project or healthy snack.

3 On a separate sheet of paper, use your prewriting plan to write a procedural composition, or plan and write a new procedural composition for something you do every day.

Research Report: Prewriting

A **research report** uses facts and details from outside sources to inform readers about a topic.

Prewriting

- First, choose a topic for your research report.
- Then do research about your topic. Jot down notes on index cards.
- Using your notes, make an outline to organize your report. Each main topic in your outline will be a paragraph in your report.

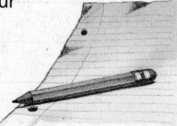

Outline

I. **Bald eagle**
   A. Called "America's bird"
   B. Seen on pictures, coins, flags

II. **Threats to bald eagles**
   A. Hurt by use of pesticide called DDT
   B. Disappeared in some parts of U.S.
   C. EPA – only 412 pairs in U.S. in 1950

III. **How bald eagles were saved**
   A. Listed as endangered in 1967
   B. Government banned DDT
   C. About 115,000 eagles in U.S. by 1990s
   D. Taken off endangered list in 2007

Name _____

Follow your teacher's directions to complete the activity.

1

Outline

I. _____

   A. _____

   B. _____

   C. _____

II. _____

   A. _____

   B. _____

   C. _____

III. _____

   A. _____

   B. _____

   C. _____

2 On a separate sheet of paper, create an outline like the one above. Then outline the main ideas and supporting facts and details that you will use in a report about an endangered animal.

3 On a separate sheet of paper, prewrite an outline for a research report. You can also use what you have learned to improve an old outline.

Research Report

A **research report** gives information about a topic. It uses outside sources for facts and details.

Parts of a Research Report

- An introduction to the report
- Facts and details that support a main idea
- Information from different sources, such as books, magazines, and the Internet
- The names of the sources that provided information
- A conclusion that sums up the main points

Introduction
Tells what the report will be about

The bald eagle has been called "America's bird." This beautiful animal is seen on pictures, coins, and flags. However, not long ago real-life bald eagles almost disappeared from the United States. It took many years of hard work to save them.

Main Idea

The United States Department of the Interior says that for years bald eagles and their eggs were hurt by DDT, a pesticide. Before long, the birds had almost disappeared in some parts of the country. Finally, **in 1967,** the government listed eagles as endangered. This protected the birds from hunters and other enemies. **Then** the government banned DDT.

Facts
Support the main idea

Information Source
Tells where paraphrased information was found

These steps helped the birds come back. According to the Environmental Protection Agency, there were 412 pairs of bald eagles in the United States in 1950. By the 1990s, though, there were almost 115,000 eagles in this country.

Conclusion
Sums up the main idea

Because the bald eagle has done so well, it was taken off the endangered list in 2007. Today, its future is looking good.

Other Transitions
First
After
In addition
Since
As a result
In the end
According to

Name _____

Follow your teacher's directions to complete the frame.

We Do 1

(Introduction) _____
_____.

(Main idea, factual details) _____
_____
_____
_____
_____
_____

(Main idea, factual details) _____
_____
_____
_____
_____
_____

In conclusion, _____
_____
_____

You Do 2 On a separate sheet of paper, write a research report about an endangered animal.

You Do 3 On a separate sheet of paper, use your prewriting plan to write a research report, or plan and write a report about a new technology.

Response to Fiction

A **response to fiction** is a composition that explains a writer's thoughts and feelings about a piece of literature. The response can be about a novel, story, or play.

Parts of a Response to Fiction

- An introduction that states the writer's opinion
- Reasons that explain the writer's opinion
- Examples from the text that support the reasons
- A conclusion that sums up the ideas

Introduction
States the writer's opinion

Supporting Sentences
Give reasons for the opinion

Examples
Support the reasons

Conclusion
Sums up the ideas

"Stormalong," by Mary Pope Osborne, tells the story of a great character. Alfred Bulltop Stormalong, called Stormy, is a giant. He is giant in size but in other ways, too.

First, Stormy's actions are bigger than life. He is a great adventurer. He goes to sea, grows millions of potatoes in Kansas, and then goes back to sea and travels all over the world.

In addition, Stormy's courage is as large as his size. For example, he battles a huge octopus and survives terrible storms.

Stormy is a giant who is adventurous and courageous. **Because of this**, I think he is a character that anyone would enjoy reading about.

Character Words
thoughtful
shy
gentle
honest
loyal
humorous
wise
clever

Name _____

Follow your teacher's directions to complete the frame.

One of the most interesting characters I've ever read about in a story is

_____ .

For instance, _____

_____ .

_____

_____

_____

_____ . In addition, _____

_____

_____

_____

_____ .

Because of this, _____

_____

_____ .

On a separate sheet of paper, plan and write a
response to your favorite fairy tale.

On a separate sheet of paper, use your prewriting plan
to write a response to fiction, or plan and write a new
response about a book, story, or character you really
enjoyed.

Journal Entry

A **journal entry** is an item written in a journal or diary. A journal entry explores the writer's experiences, thoughts, and feelings. It can include daily observations, facts, and important personal experiences.

Parts of a Journal Entry

- A beginning that introduces the topic
- Facts about what happened, when it happened, who was involved, and where they were
- Vivid details that come from the five senses
- An ending that tells what the writer learned or how the event ended

Beginning
Tells what the entry is about

Facts
Tell who, what, where, when, why

Sensory Details
Include sights, sounds, smells, tastes, and feelings

Ending
Tells how the event ended and how the writer felt

August 14, 2012

Today I went to my grandmother's house and she taught me how to bake bread. I was a little bit nervous because she is a great cook and I'd never made bread before. I asked Nona to share her bread recipe because someday I might want to pass it on to my own children.

First, Nona let me mix the ingredients, which included flour, yeast, milk, oil, water, and salt. She showed me how to knead the dough by squeezing and mashing it. **Then** we put the bowl of dough on a windowsill where it rose and doubled in size. **Next**, I shaped the dough and put it in bread pans. In the oven, the dough turned golden brown. When the bread was done, we ate warm slices with melted butter. Yum! Nona said that I did a good job. I feel proud that now I can make bread like Nona does.

Other Transitions
Because
After
During
Now
Before
Later
Last
Soon
Earlier

Name _____

Follow your teacher's directions to complete the frame.

We Do 1

_____

_____

_____

_____

At first _____

_____

_____. Then _____

_____

_____. Next, _____

_____

Finally, _____

_____

_____

_____. I felt _____

_____

_____

You Do 2 On a separate sheet of paper, write a journal entry
about a time you were surprised.

You Do 3 On a separate sheet of paper, use your prewriting plan
to write a journal entry, or make a new plan to write
about a holiday you will never forget.

Public Service Announcement

A **public service announcement** is an advertisement that gives helpful information to the community. Public service announcements appear on radio and television and in newspapers and magazines.

Parts of a Public Service Announcement

- An introduction that grabs the audience's attention
- Facts that give helpful information about the topic
- A call to action that urges the audience to do something
- A conclusion that persuades the audience to feel and act a certain way

Introduction
Gets the reader to pay attention

School is back in session in Green Valley. Be smart! Pay attention to school bus safety.

Facts
Tell about the topic

Did you know that, in this country, about 17,000 students are injured every year just riding the bus to school? They are treated for cuts, sprains, and bruises.

What can you do to have a safe ride? Here are some simple steps:

- **First**, use the handrail while you get on the bus.
- Buckle your seat belt **as soon as** you sit.
- **During** the trip, talk quietly. Don't distract the driver.
- Only stand up **after** the bus has completely stopped.

Call to Action
Includes specific things for the audience to do

Other Transitions
Before
Next
Until
Immediately
As soon as
Meanwhile
Later
Last

Conclusion
Persuades the audience to take part

Green Valley students deserve a safe ride to school. Be sure to follow these safety rules every time you ride the bus.

Name _____

Follow your teacher's directions to complete the frame.

We Do 1

_____

_____

_____

_____

- First, _____

_____

- Then _____

_____

- Next, _____

_____

- Finally, _____

_____

_____

_____

_____

You Do 2 On a separate sheet of paper, write a public service announcement to persuade people in your community to help clean up a local park.

You Do 3 On a separate sheet of paper, use your prewriting plan to write a public service announcement, or make a new plan for an announcement persuading classmates to make your school better in some way.

Opinion Essay: Prewriting

An **opinion essay** gives the writer's beliefs about a topic. It uses facts and details to explain the writer's opinions.

Prewriting for Opinion Essay

- Brainstorm a list of topics that are important to you. Choose one that you have a strong opinion about.
- Jot down reasons that support your opinion. Think about facts and details that will explain each reason.
- Now use a graphic organizer to plan your opinion essay.

Opinion: Most important invention is the telephone

Reason: It helps us communicate.

Facts and details:

Use it to call friends, family, police, fire department. Use it to make plans, share news, and get help.

Reason: It helps us learn.

Facts and details:

Surf Internet. Look at maps or a dictionary.

Reason: It entertains us.

Facts and details:

Play games. Watch movies. Listen to music.

Name _____

Follow your teacher's directions to complete the activity.

 1 Opinion: _____

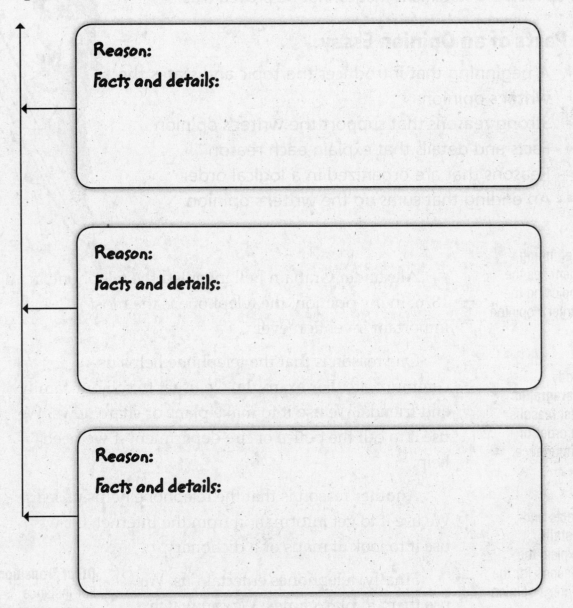

Reason:
Facts and details:

Reason:
Facts and details:

Reason:
Facts and details:

2 On a separate sheet of paper, fill in a graphic organizer like the one above. Write your opinion and reasons that support it. Explain your reasons with facts and details.

3 On a separate sheet of paper, prewrite an opinion essay. You can also use what you have learned to improve an old plan.

Opinion Essay

An **opinion essay** expresses the writer's beliefs about a topic. An opinion is a statement that cannot be proved true.

Parts of an Opinion Essay

- A beginning that introduces the topic and states the writer's opinion
- Strong reasons that support the writer's opinion
- Facts and details that explain each reason
- Reasons that are organized in a logical order
- An ending that sums up the writer's opinion

Beginning
Identifies the topic and the writer's opinion

Body Paragraphs
List reasons in order of importance

Facts and Details
Explain the reasons for the writer's opinion

Ending
Tells why your opinion makes sense

Alexander Graham Bell invented the telephone in 1876. In my opinion, the telephone is the most important invention ever.

One reason is that the telephone helps us communicate. **For example**, we use it to call our family and friends. We use it to make plans or share news. We use it to call the police or fire department if we need help.

Another reason is that the telephone helps us learn. We use it to get information from the Internet. Or we use it to look at maps or a dictionary.

Finally, telephones entertain us. We use them to play games. We can watch movies on them. We can **also** use them to listen to music.

Can you imagine life without a phone? This invention fits in a pocket. But it connects us to the whole world.

Other Transitions
For instance
In order to
Most importantly
Mainly
In addition
Most significant
Least important
In fact

Follow your teacher's directions to complete the frame.

I believe that _____

_____

_____.

One reason is that _____

_____

_____

_____

Second, _____

_____

_____.

Finally, _____

_____

_____. For example, _____

_____

In conclusion, _____.

_____

_____

On a separate sheet of paper, write an opinion essay about another invention that you think is important. Be sure to support your opinion with strong reasons.

On a separate sheet of paper, use your prewriting plan to write an opinion essay, or make a new plan to write about a custom or tradition you feel strongly about.

Prewriting

The **writing process** is a strategy that can help you write. It has five stages: prewriting, drafting, revising, editing, and publishing. **Prewriting** is the first stage.

How to Prewrite

- Prewriting means planning before you write.
- First, think about your TAP: task, audience, and purpose.
- Plan by brainstorming ideas to write about.
- Some ways to brainstorm include making lists, clustering, or looking through your journal.
- After you brainstorm, choose one idea to write about. Circle it.
- Gather information on your chosen idea, or topic.
- Put the information in order.

1 **Decide your TAP.**

Task	persuasive essay
Audience	principal
Purpose	persuade about ideas

2 **Brainstorm a list.**

- flea market
- car wash
- fair
- field day

3 **Gather information.**

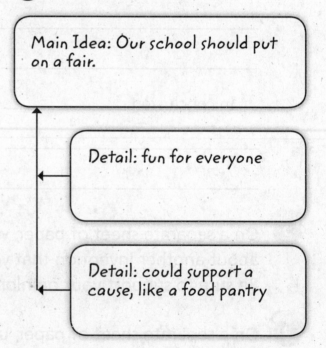

Main Idea: Our school should put on a fair.

Detail: fun for everyone

Detail: could support a cause, like a food pantry

4 Organize the information.

Story Chart for Narratives

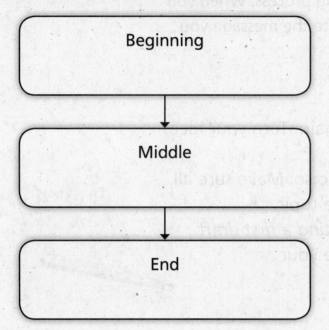

Chart for How-to Paragraphs

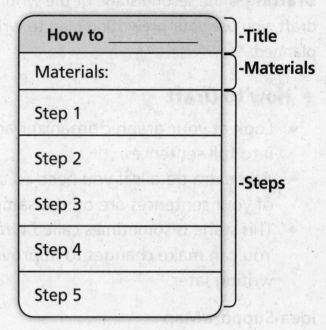

Venn Diagram to Compare and Contrast

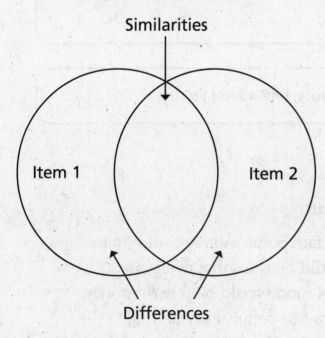

Outlines for Reports

Topic
I. Main Idea
   A. Detail
   B. Detail
   C. Detail
II. Main Idea
   A. Detail
   B. Detail
III. Conclusion

Drafting

Drafting is the second stage of the writing process. When you draft, you use your prewriting plan to write the message you planned.

✏️ How to Draft

- Look at your graphic organizer again. Turn your ideas into full sentences.
- Add extra details if you need to do so. Make sure all of your sentences are on the same topic.
- This stage is sometimes called *writing a first draft*. You can make changes to improve your writing later.

Idea-Support Map

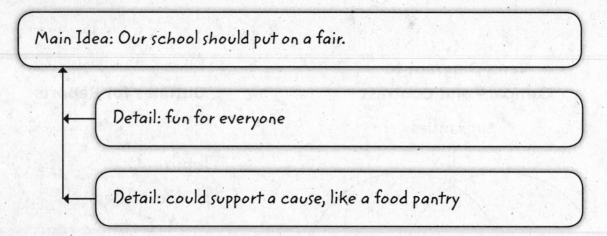

Main Idea: Our school should put on a fair.

Detail: fun for everyone

Detail: could support a cause, like a food pantry

Draft

Our school should put on a fair. Some money could go to the local food pantry. There should be rides that everyone likes, like the Ferris wheel. Good food would help earn money, too. We could also give money to our community animal shelter. There are many good causes. The fair would have many things to do. It would be fun for everyone!

Venn Diagram

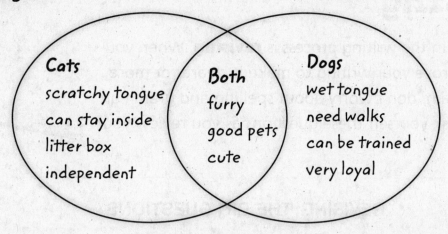

Cats
scratchy tongue
can stay inside
litter box
independent

Both
furry
good pets
cute

Dogs
wet tongue
need walks
can be trained
very loyal

Draft

Dogs and cats make great pets, and they're both so furry and cute. But there are some differences, too. Cats can stay inside all the time and they use a litter box. Dogs need walks. Cats are quite independent. Dogs can be trained to do tricks and are very loyal.

Outline

Amazon Rainforest
    I. Size of the rainforest
        A. Covers 2.5 square miles
        B. 2/3 of the South American continent

Draft

The Amazon Rainforest is the largest rainforest in the world. It covers 2.5 million square miles. That's larger than the United States, if you don't count Alaska and Hawaii! The Amazon Rainforest covers two-thirds of the whole continent.

Revising

The next stage in the writing process is **revising**. When you revise, you improve your writing to make it clearer or more interesting. Again, don't worry about spelling and grammar mistakes yet. Ask yourself these questions as you review your working draft:

REVISING: THE BIG QUESTIONS

- Did I say what I wanted to say?
- Did I elaborate and use details?
- Did I organize the facts, events, or ideas clearly?
- Did I write in an interesting way that suits my audience?

Ways to Revise

- Use editor's marks to show your changes.
- Combine words or sentences to make your ideas flow smoothly.

Editor's Marks
≡ Make a capital.
∧ Insert.
ℓ Delete.
⊙ Make a period.
∧ Insert a comma.
/ Make lowercase.

Some money could go to good causes. ~~Some money could go to~~ the local food pantry. *such as*

Some money could go to good causes, such as the local food pantry.

- Change words or add modifiers and sensory words to make your ideas clear.

carnival *really exciting*
The rides are ~~good~~.

The carnival rides are really exciting.

- Take out unnecessary words or information.

The money we earn could go to good causes. I hear the food pantry is in danger of closing. ~~We should also have good food.~~

- Add ideas or details to make your writing stronger.

Draft: The fair would have many things to do. It would be fun.

Revision: What better way is there to spend time and energy? We would all work hard and have a wonderful time as well.

Here's how a revised draft might look:

First Draft

Our school should put on a fair. Some ~~money~~ could
*The money we earn could be donated to any number
of good causes.*
go to the local food pantry. ~~There should be rides that~~
~~everyone likes, like the Ferris wheel. Good food would~~
I hear it is in danger of closing.
~~help earn money, too.~~ We could also give money to our
community animal shelter. ~~There are many good causes.~~
What better way is there to spend
~~The fair would have many things to do. It would be fun~~
time and energy? We would all work hard for charity and
have a wonderful time as well.
~~for everyone!~~

Editing

Editing, or proofreading for errors, is the fourth stage of the writing process.

✏ Editing

- Check for mistakes in punctuation, capitalization, spelling, and grammar. You can use a dictionary and a grammar book to help.
- Make sure your paragraphs are indented.
- Use editing marks to show corrections on your paper.
- Use the spelling and grammar checker if you are working on a computer. Be sure to double-check your work for errors the checker won't catch.

Editor's Marks

≡ Make a capital.
∧ Insert.
⌇ Delete.
⊙ Make a period.
⌄ Insert a comma.
/ Make lowercase.

Revised Draft

Dear Principal Martinez,

The key to a great ~~far~~ fair is good food and ~~exsiting~~ exciting rides. That's what makes people come out and spend money⊙ Our school could rent a Ferris wheel∧ a giant slide, and maybe some other rides, too. ~~w~~e could pay back the rental fees from the money ~~erned~~ earned at the fair. Food would be easy. Students and parents could work together to make ~~delishus~~ delicious food to sell. As you can see, I don't think rides or food for the fair would be a problem.

Sincerely,
Amanda

Publishing

The last stage of the writing process is **publishing**. Before you publish, you can go back to any stage to fix or improve your writing.

- Decide how you want to publish. You might publish by sharing a written piece, giving an oral report, or giving a multimedia presentation.
- Type or write a clean copy of your piece.
- When you give a presentation, write note cards with the main ideas to guide your oral reporting or multimedia presentation.
- If you use multimedia, use a computer to choose pictures, charts, audio, or video to go with your writing.

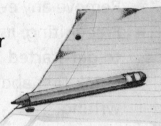

Why We Should Have a School Fair
by Amanda Fleming

I believe our school should put on a fair. The money we earn could be donated to any number of good causes. Some could go to the local food pantry. We could also give money to our community animal shelter. I hear they're in danger of closing. What better way is there to spend our time and energy? We would be learning a lot about planning, budgets, and cooperating as a school. Just think, we would all be working hard for charity while having a wonderful time!

Evidence

Evidence, organization, purpose, elaboration, development, and conventions are the six writing traits. These traits are found in all good writing. **Evidence** is the details, examples, and facts you include in informative and persuasive writing.

Evidence

- Do research to find facts, examples, and details.
- Remove any evidence that does not support your topic.
- Freewriting, listing, and discussing are good ways to get started.
- Think first about why and for whom you are writing.

Freewriting Sample

I want to persuade my friends to start a baseball team. So much fun, good exercise. If we started a baseball team, we could play every week. We could get better at sports and have our own t-shirts.

Freewriting Tips

- Just write what comes to mind.
- Don't worry about grammar or punctuation.
- Review your free-writing and circle important ideas.

Listing

Topic: Baseball Team

Details:

-- fun 1

-- good exercise 2

-- play every week

-- better at sports 3

-- have our own t-shirts

Informative Writing

- Make a list of details you already know about a topic.
- Make a list of questions you have about the topic.
- Research your topic.
- Possible graphic organizers: web, note cards, timeline

An octopus has many skills to defend itself.

-- can change color

-- can shoot ink

-- can use tools such as shells to hide

Source: Animal Encyclopedia

Persuasive Writing

- Write your goal or opinion.
- Research facts to support your goal or opinion.
- Possible graphic organizer: column chart

Book Fair		
reason: promote reading	reason: fundraising	reason: have fun!
details: many books; earn prizes	details: sell books; earn money for library	details: help each other find books & games

Organization

Organization is the order in which you present your ideas. Different kinds of writing need different kinds of organization.

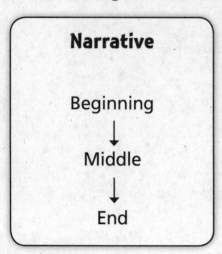

Narrative

Beginning
↓
Middle
↓
End

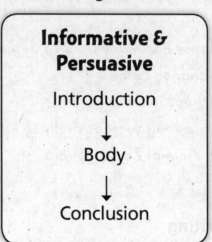

Informative & Persuasive

Introduction
↓
Body
↓
Conclusion

Narrative Writing

- Chronological, or sequential, order: the events told in the order in which they happen
- A beginning that grabs readers' interest
- A middle with interesting details about the events
- An ending that tells how the story worked out or how the writer felt

Beginning → Julie heard a *thump!* She thought she imagined it at first, but then there it was again! It sounded like it was coming from downstairs. She crept out of bed and to the top of the stairs to listen. *Thump! Thump!* Julie was terrified! She thought maybe someone was stomping

Middle → around downstairs, but she knew her parents and her little brother were in bed asleep. Who could it be? Her heart began to race as she went down the stairs slowly to see what was happening. Then she heard a jingle that sounded like the bell on her pet rabbit's water bottle.

End → She flipped on the light and saw the culprit: Sadie the rabbit was sitting in her cage, stomping her foot. Julie was relieved. Mystery solved!

Informative Writing

- Information presented in a logical order
- An introduction that grabs readers' attention
- A body that presents information, explains ideas, or defines important terms
- Facts and examples, often from outside sources
- A conclusion that summarizes the information

Introduction →

Body →

Conclusion →

Depending on who you ask, rabbits can be good luck or bad luck. But what are these animals really like? Well, rabbits are small mammals. They have long ears, strong hind legs, and short tails. Rabbits scare easily and stomp their feet to keep danger away. These animals are pretty smart.

Persuasive Writing

- An introduction, body, and conclusion like informative writing
- Reasons presented in a logical order, such as least to most important

Reasons →

Rabbits make the best house pets! First, they are cute and have soft fur that is nice to pet. Second, rabbits are playful. They like to hop on shelves, run through tunnels, and play with balls and other toys. Some can even be taught to do tricks! But the most important reason of all is that rabbits are very friendly. A rabbit could be a great companion for anyone, young or old. I would love to have a rabbit as a pet!

Purpose

Purpose is the reason you are writing. Your purpose will help you figure out who your audience is.

- Your purpose for writing will change, depending on your readers and your reasons for writing.
- If your reason for writing is to persuade or inform, you will most likely use formal language. Formal words make your writing sound serious.
- If your reason for writing is to tell a story or to entertain, you might use informal language. Informal words make your writing sound funny or realistic.

Sample Informal Letter

Dear James,

    That's awesome that you won the spelling bee! If I were you, I would have been totally anxious up on stage. I guess you studied like crazy and really knew the words. Anyway, congrats!

          Your friend,
          Amy

Words and phrases like *awesome* and *like crazy* sound like natural speech.

Sample Formal Letter

Dear Mr. Chen,

    Thank you for donating gift certificates to your bookstore to the winners of the Washington Elementary School Sixteenth Annual Spelling Bee. The students really appreciated the prizes! We look forward to shopping at your store.

          Sincerely,
          James Douglas

Thank you, *appreciated*, and *we look forward* are examples of more formal language.

Elaboration

How you choose to elaborate on the ideas and details in your writing helps create a picture in your reader's mind. Writers use **exact words** to make their writing more meaningful and interesting.

> During the summer, I <u>swim</u> every morning. It's so <u>refreshing</u> to <u>dive</u> into the water on a <u>hot</u>, <u>sticky</u> day. I <u>blow bubbles</u> under the <u>surface</u> and <u>jump</u> up only when I need more air.

> On Sundays we go,
> <u>Grandma</u> and I,
> To pick <u>wild berries</u>
> And <u>bake</u> one big pie.
> I wash the fruit,
> She <u>molds</u> the <u>crust</u>.
> Once it's all done,
> She says, "Try it. You must!"

As you revise, look for unclear or boring words. Ask yourself these questions:

- Do my **verbs** show exactly what is happening?
- Are the people, places, and things easy for my readers to see? Do the **nouns** create a clear picture?
- Are there **other words** I can add or change?

Not Exact:

After school Jeff and I <u>went</u> to the <u>store</u>. The smell of <u>nice</u> bread filled the air. We <u>got a bunch of stuff</u> for the picnic.

Exact:

After school Jeff and I <u>biked</u> to the <u>delicatessen</u>. The smell of <u>fresh</u> bread filled the air. We <u>bought tuna sandwiches</u> for the picnic.

Try replacing dull or unclear words with new vocabulary words.

Development

Good writers **develop** narratives with interesting details and clear descriptions.

- Describe characters and settings using interesting words and descriptions.
- Develop events and experiences that describe conflicts and how they are resolved in the story.
- Write different kinds of sentences that begin in different ways.

"Tomorrow is going to be a great day," thought Zack <u>as he was getting ready for bed</u>. <u>The next day was a school holiday</u>. Zack planned to ride bikes with his friend Luis. The weather was supposed to be clear and mild, <u>a picture perfect day to ride to the park</u>.

The writer described what the character did as he thought about the next day's event.

This phrase helps the reader understand the sequence of events.

This description and expression help the reader visualize the kind of weather that was expected.

Use a variety of sentence beginnings.

Too Many Sentences Beginning the Same Way

Hailey looked at her art project. She picked up her paintbrush. She added one more stroke of red. She put the brush down. She thought, "Now I am ready for the art show."

Varied Beginnings

Hailey looked at her art project. Then she picked up a paintbrush and added one more stroke of red. After setting her brush down, she thought, "Now I am ready for the art show."

Use different sentence lengths.

Too Many Sentences of the Same Length

Baseball is a popular sport around the world. Many towns and schools in other countries have started baseball programs. Children are now able to play on organized teams. Girls and boys can both join Little League teams here in the US. They can easily play on the same teams.

Varied Lengths

Baseball is a popular sport around the world. Since many towns and schools in other countries have started baseball programs, children are now able to play on organized teams. Both girls and boys can play together on organized Little League teams in the US.

Use different kinds of sentences.

Similar Sentences

Snails are slimy creatures. They carry their houses on their backs. They live in many kinds of places. Some of these are on the land, in the ocean, or in freshwater lakes.

Varied Sentences

What is a slimy creature that carries its house on its back? It's a snail! Snails live in many kinds of places. Some of these are on the land, in the ocean, or in freshwater lakes.

Conventions

Conventions are rules about grammar, spelling, punctuation, and capitalization. One way to make sure you are following the rules when you write or edit is to have an editing checklist.

Sample Editing Checklist

Punctuation

____ Did I use correct end punctuation in my sentences?

____ Did I use commas correctly in compound sentences?

____ Did I use quotation marks correctly?

Capitalization

____ Did I start every sentence with a capital letter?

____ Did I capitalize proper nouns?

Spelling

____ Did I spell all of my words correctly?

Grammar

____ Did my sentences have correct subject-verb agreement?

____ Did I avoid run-on sentences and fragments?

Common Errors

Fragments and Run-Ons

A sentence should have a **subject** and a **verb**. It starts with a capital letter and ends with a period.

Wrong Way	Right Way
The sheep in the field.	The sheep in the field are ready to be sheared.
Can shear them to gather the wool.	The farmers can shear them to gather the wool.
Wool made from sheep was one of the first textiles people around the world make clothing from wool.	Wool made from sheep was one of the first textiles. People around the world make clothing from wool.

Compound and Complex Sentences

A **compound sentence** combines two sentences. The clauses are separated by a comma and a coordinating conjunction. A **complex sentence** has an independent and a dependent clause and does not need a comma.

Wrong Way	Right Way
The barn is only half-painted but it already looks great!	The barn is only half-painted, but it already looks great!
The cows are fed, after they are milked.	The cows are fed after they are milked.

Subject-Verb Agreement

Make sure the subject and verb of your sentence agree.

Wrong Way	Right Way
Joan plant tree in the schoolyard.	Joan plants a tree in the schoolyard.
José and Marisol paints a mural near the playground.	José and Marisol paint a mural near the playground.
The students wants to make recess better.	The students want to make recess better.

Possessives

Use an apostrophe to show that a noun is possessive.

Wrong Way	Right Way
That is Barrys football.	That is Barry's football.
Alexs mother brings sandwiches and juice to our game's.	Alex's mother brings sandwiches and juice to our games.
All the boy's new jerseys are red.	All the boys' new jerseys are red.

Writing Workshop

In a **writing workshop**, writers read each other's work. Then they ask questions about the work or suggest changes. The goal of a workshop is to make everyone's writing better.

How a Writing Workshop Works

- Give everyone a copy of your revised draft.
- Read your writing aloud, or have everyone in the group read silently.
- Listen attentively and take notes.
- Point out the good qualities in your classmates' work.
- Ask questions if something is confusing.
- Politely and respectfully suggest ways to improve writing.

I know we have to make up extra snow days. I think we should make them up during spring break instead of in June. Making up days during spring break will keep students focused. Also, we will still get a few days to relax. Spring break is great, but getting out of school early in June is better. Summer already seems too short. If we have to make up three days, that is actually five more days of June spent in school. Please consider changing the make-up policy. Students will thank you.

> Add a transition word—maybe <u>however.</u>

> What do you mean by <u>focused</u>?

> What makes getting out early in June "better"?

> How do 3 make-up days turn into 5?

> Your paragraph is organized well!

Guide for a Writing Workshop

The Writer's Job

- ☐ Give a copy of your writing to each of the classmates in your workshop.
- ☐ Read your paper aloud or introduce your writing and let classmates read it silently.
- ☐ Ask for comments and listen carefully. Keep an open mind.
- ☐ Take notes or write down suggestions to help you remember.
- ☐ Ask for advice about anything you had trouble with.
- ☐ Reread your paper after the workshop.
- ☐ Use your notes to revise and make changes.

The Responder's Job

- ☐ Be kind, respectful, positive, polite, and helpful.
- ☐ Listen to or read the writing carefully.
- ☐ Make notes about the writing.
- ☐ Retell what you have heard.
- ☐ Tell at least two things that you liked about the writing. Be specific.
- ☐ Ask questions about things you don't understand.
- ☐ Give one or two suggestions to help the writer.

Negative/Unhelpful Responses	Positive/Helpful Responses
Why are your details so dull?	What exciting details could you add?
Where's the ending?	What new way can you end the story?
Why didn't you tell more about your character?	What is your character like?

Using the Internet

A computer is a great tool for writing. You can use a computer to look for facts.

- A search engine will help you find websites about your topic. If you are not sure whether a particular website is a good source, ask your teacher.
- Online encyclopedias have lots of useful facts.
- Be sure to record your sources as you do research so that you can reference and credit them later.

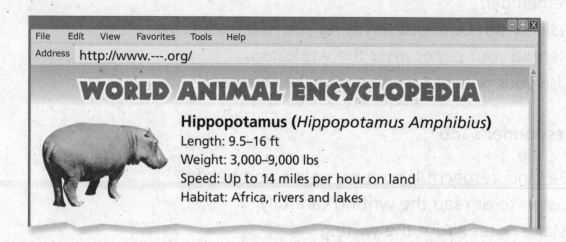

File   Edit   View   Favorites   Tools   Help

Address   http://www.----.org/

WORLD ANIMAL ENCYCLOPEDIA

Hippopotamus (*Hippopotamus Amphibius*)
Length: 9.5–16 ft
Weight: 3,000–9,000 lbs
Speed: Up to 14 miles per hour on land
Habitat: Africa, rivers and lakes

Facts:
- 9.5–16 ft.
- 3,000–9,000 lbs.
- moves up to 15 mph
- lives in Africa

Draft:

The Hippo
by Alice Chase

The hippopotamus can be up to 16 feet long and can weigh from 3,000 to 9,000 pounds. It lives in rivers and lakes in Africa. The hippo goes at a slow pace of no more than 15 miles per hour.

You can use online encyclopedias to find facts for your writing.

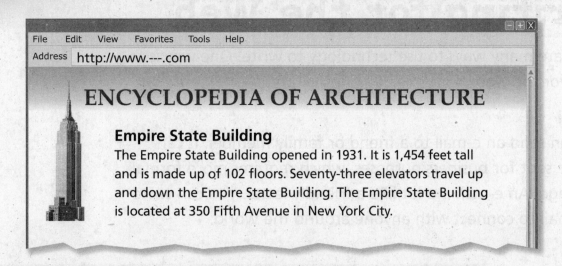

File   Edit   View   Favorites   Tools   Help
Address http://www.---.com

ENCYCLOPEDIA OF ARCHITECTURE

Empire State Building
The Empire State Building opened in 1931. It is 1,454 feet tall and is made up of 102 floors. Seventy-three elevators travel up and down the Empire State Building. The Empire State Building is located at 350 Fifth Avenue in New York City.

Facts:

- opened in 1931
- 102 floors
- 73 elevators

Source: "Empire State Building." Encyclopedia of Architecture. Web. 24 Feb. 2012. www.---.com

Don't forget to note the source!

File   Edit   View   Favorites   Tools   Help
Address http://www.---.org

Flower Encyclopedia

Rudbeckia hirta
(Common nickname: Black-eyed Susan)
Maximum height: 1 meter
Region: most of North America
Appearance: brown center, yellow petals

Facts:

- max height: 1 meter
- North America
- state flower of Maryland

Source: "Rudbeckia hirta." Flower Encyclopedia. Web. 28 Nov. 2012. www.---.com

Writing for the Web

There are many ways to use technology to write. One way is to write for the web.

E-mail

You can send an e-mail to a friend or family member. It can also be sent for business purposes, which requires more formal language. An e-mail is a lot like a friendly letter. You can write an e-mail to connect with anyone around the world.

Heading
Includes the recipient's **e-mail address** and a **subject line**

To sal@---.com

Subject My trip to Chicago

Beginning
Tells why you are writing

Dear Uncle Sal,

Thanks for your message! I really liked hearing about your trip to Japan. I just got back from a trip, too. I went with Mom and Tony to Chicago for vacation.

Middle
Tells what happened

We saw so many cool things! The first day, we went to this huge aquarium. My favorite part was seeing the sharks. They're even bigger than I thought they would be! The next day, we went to Millennium Park and saw this big silver sculpture that looks like a giant bean! Tony and I made faces at it and saw our reflections. It was pretty weird. The last day we went to Navy Pier and I rode on a huge Ferris wheel. I could see the whole city from the top! It was a really great trip. I can't wait to hear back from you! I want to learn more about Japan.

End
Wraps up the message

Your nephew,
Johnny

Blog Post

Blog is short for "weblog." It is a journal that you keep on the Internet so that other people can read and comment. One way to use a blog is to share news about yourself or your friends and family with others. Blogs can also be essays or include opinions.

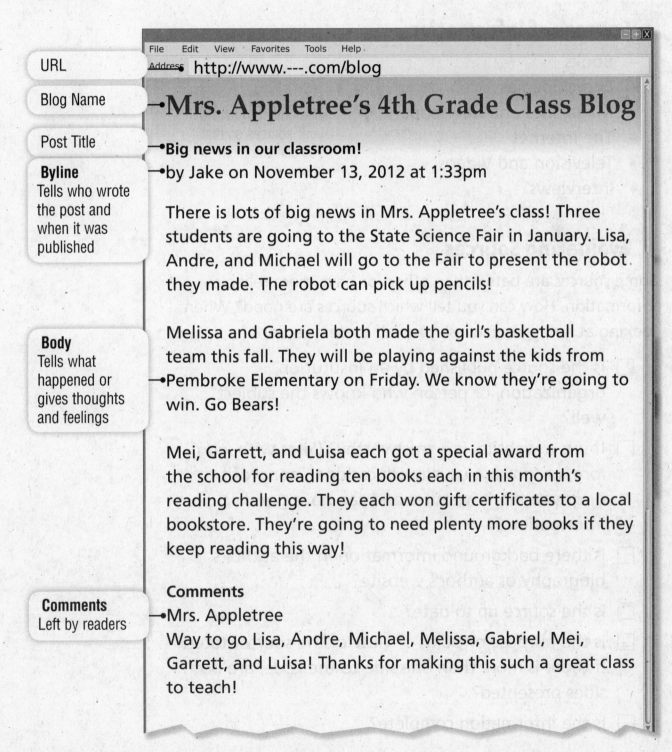

URL

Blog Name

Post Title

Byline
Tells who wrote the post and when it was published

Body
Tells what happened or gives thoughts and feelings

Comments
Left by readers

File   Edit   View   Favorites   Tools   Help

Address   http://www.---.com/blog

Mrs. Appletree's 4th Grade Class Blog

Big news in our classroom!

by Jake on November 13, 2012 at 1:33pm

There is lots of big news in Mrs. Appletree's class! Three students are going to the State Science Fair in January. Lisa, Andre, and Michael will go to the Fair to present the robot they made. The robot can pick up pencils!

Melissa and Gabriela both made the girl's basketball team this fall. They will be playing against the kids from Pembroke Elementary on Friday. We know they're going to win. Go Bears!

Mei, Garrett, and Luisa each got a special award from the school for reading ten books each in this month's reading challenge. They each won gift certificates to a local bookstore. They're going to need plenty more books if they keep reading this way!

Comments

Mrs. Appletree
Way to go Lisa, Andre, Michael, Melissa, Gabriel, Mei, Garrett, and Luisa! Thanks for making this such a great class to teach!

Doing Research

The best way to support your points in your informative or persuasive writing is to use facts and details. The best way to find facts and details is to do research.

Sources of Information

- Books
- Encyclopedias
- Magazines and Newspapers
- The Internet
- Television and Videos
- Interviews

> Remember to record your sources so that you can cite them later.

Evaluating Sources

Some sources are better than others or have more reliable information. How can you tell which sources are good? When looking at a new source, ask yourself these questions:

- ☐ Is the source published by an institution, organization, or person who knows the subject well?

- ☐ If it is a website, is it trustworthy? (Sites with .edu, .org, or .gov are usually educational, nonprofit, or government websites and can have good information.)

- ☐ Is there background information in the author's biography or author's website?

- ☐ Is the source up to date?

- ☐ Is the purpose or point of view of the source stated? If there is more than one side to the issue, are both sides presented?

- ☐ Is the information complete?

Finding Information

One way to find information is to search in your library's electronic card catalog or use an Internet search engine. In order to find good sources of information, you need to search using good keywords.

A **keyword** is a word or phrase about a subject. A good keyword to start with might be the topic of your research.

Tips:

- Narrow your topic down to a specific keyword. If you pick something too broad, your search will get hundreds of results.
- Don't pick anything too specific or you won't find enough results to get enough information.

Less Effective Keywords	Effective Keywords
cars	the first car
old cars	Model T
inventors	Henry Ford
Grandma's red 1957 Chevy	1957 Chevys

Parts of a Nonfiction Book

- A **table of contents** shows how the book is organized and lists names and page numbers of chapters
- A **glossary** gives definitions of special words used in the book
- A **bibliography** lists sources the author used when writing the book
- An **index** is an alphabetical list of topics covered in the book

Notetaking

You will find a great deal of information when you research.
One way to keep track of it and stay organized is to take notes.

✎ Note Cards

You can take notes on your research in two ways.

1. You can write a main idea or a research question at the top of the card. Then write details or the answer to your research question below. At the bottom, include your source.

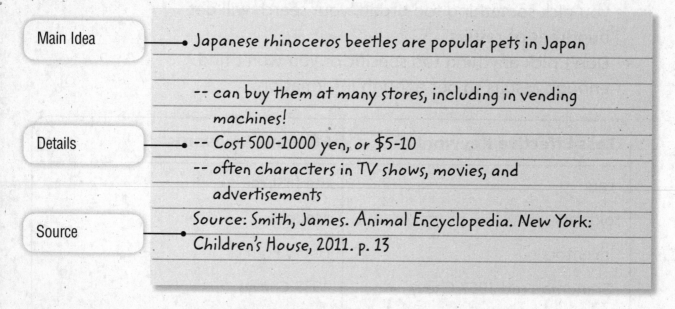

Main Idea —→ Japanese rhinoceros beetles are popular pets in Japan

Details —→
-- can buy them at many stores, including in vending machines!
-- Cost 500-1000 yen, or $5-10
-- often characters in TV shows, movies, and advertisements

Source —→ Source: Smith, James. Animal Encyclopedia. New York: Children's House, 2011. p. 13

2. You can write your research question at the top and then include a direct quote from the source.

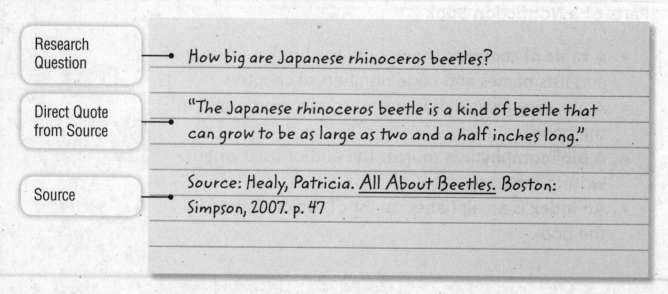

Research Question —→ How big are Japanese rhinoceros beetles?

Direct Quote from Source —→ "The Japanese rhinoceros beetle is a kind of beetle that can grow to be as large as two and a half inches long."

Source —→ Source: Healy, Patricia. All About Beetles. Boston: Simpson, 2007. p. 47

Writing to Learn

Think-Aloud on Paper

- As you read, write notes about what you are reading.
- Write notes on what you understand about the topic.
- You might write notes on what images you picture as you read, what you predict will happen in a story, or how what you read is like something you have experienced.

Learning Logs

- A learning log is a place for you to comment on, ask questions about, or make connections to your reading.
- In the "Note-Taking" column, write the exact words you read.
- In the "Note-Making" column, write your reactions to or questions about what you read.

Learning Log: "Starting a Garden"	
Note-Taking	Note-Making
"Plant seeds in the spring." "Choose good plants for your garden." "You should see sprouts about ten days after you plant your seeds."	What day is the best day to plant seeds? I want to plant cucumbers and tomatoes. Cucumbers are tasty. Is there anything I can do to make my plants grow faster?

Writing to a Prompt

A **prompt** is a writing assignment. Sometimes teachers give timed writing assignments for class exercises or tests.

✏️ Writing to a Prompt

- Read the prompt carefully.
- Note whether it asks you to give information, express thoughts and feelings, or persuade someone.
- Look for clues that tell what to include. For non-fiction, you might see *fact, opinion, examples, reasons*. For stories, *conflict, characters, plot*.
- Plan your writing, and then write. Restate key words from the prompt in your topic sentence.
- Some prompts have time limits. Plan how to best use your time.

Prompt: Think of a place you would like to visit. Write a paragraph explaining where you want to go and why you want to go there.

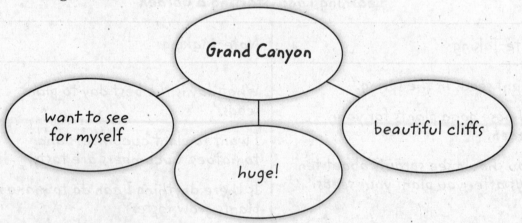

Grand Canyon

want to see for myself

huge!

beautiful cliffs

I would like to visit the Grand Canyon. My aunt Carol went to visit it last year and brought back many photos. The cliffs and rocks looked beautiful. Aunt Carol said that the Grand Canyon is even bigger in person than it looks in the photos! It does not look like any place I have ever been to before. I want to see it with my own eyes someday.

Written Prompts

A **written prompt** is a statement or question that asks you to complete a writing task. Here is an example of a written prompt that asks for a personal narrative:

> Almost everyone has had an interesting experience visiting a new place. Think about your own experience in a new place. It may have happened during a visit to another state, to a museum, or to some other place. Now tell or recount a story to your reader about what happened when you visited that place.

Here are some other examples of written prompts:

Narrative Writing	Persuasive Writing
These prompts ask you to "tell a story."	These prompts ask you to "convince" or "persuade."
Informative Writing	**Response to Literature**
These prompts may ask you to "tell or explain why."	These prompts ask you to answer questions about a piece you read.

Picture Prompts

A **picture prompt** is a statement or question about a picture. It asks you to tell something about the picture. Here is an example of a picture prompt that asks for a description.

Picture yourself in this scene. Write a composition for your teacher in which you tell what you see.

Checklists and Rubrics

A **rubric** is a chart that helps you when you write and revise.
Score 6 tells you what to aim for in your writing.

	• Focus • Support	• Organization
Score 6	My writing is focused and supported by facts or details.	My writing has a clear introduction and conclusion. Ideas are clearly organized.
Score 5	My writing is mostly focused and supported by facts or details.	My writing has an introduction and a conclusion. Ideas are mostly organized.
Score 4	My writing is mostly focused and supported by some facts or details.	My writing has an introduction and a conclusion. Most ideas are organized.
Score 3	Some of my writing is focused and supported by some facts or details.	My writing has an introduction or a conclusion, but might be missing one. Some ideas are organized.
Score 2	My writing is not focused and is supported by few facts or details.	My writing might not have an introduction or a conclusion. Few ideas are organized.
Score 1	My writing is not focused or supported by facts or details.	My writing is missing an introduction and a conclusion. Few or no ideas are organized.

• Elaboration • Purpose	• Conventions • Development • Evidence
Purpose is strong. Writing grabs readers' interest. Word choices strongly support the purpose and audience.	Writing has no errors in spelling, grammar, capitalization, or punctuation. It includes description, details, and/or reasons.
Purpose is clear. Writing holds readers' interest. Most word choices support the purpose and audience.	Writing has few errors in spelling, grammar, capitalization, or punctuation. It includes descriptions, details, and/or reasons.
Purpose is clear, but could be stronger in the beginning or end. Overall writing holds readers' interest. Word choices good.	Writing has some errors in spelling, grammar, capitalization, or punctuation. It includes some description, details, and/or reasons.
Purpose is clear at the beginning or end. Some of the writing interests readers. Few word choices support the purpose and audience.	Writing has some errors in spelling, grammar, capitalization, or punctuation. It includes a few examples of description, details, and/or reasons.
Purpose is mostly unclear. Writing does not include desciption and does not hold readers' interest. Weak word choices.	Writing has many errors in spelling, grammar, capitalization, or punctuation. Little variety of sentences. Some sentences are incomplete.
Purpose is unclear. Writing is not interesting to read.	Writing has many errors in spelling, grammar, capitalization, or punctuation.

Summary

A **summary** is a short description of the most important main ideas and details from a piece of writing.

Parts of a Summary

- An introduction that tells what the summary is about
- A body that tells about the most important parts of the text in your own words
- A conclusion that tells how the piece of writing ends

Introduction
Tells what the article is about

Body
Tells the most important parts of the article

The Nobel Peace Prize

The article "Nobel Peace Prize Winners" tells about who won the Nobel Peace Prize in 2011. It explains what the peace prize is and gives a short biography of the winners.

The Nobel Peace Prize is given to people or organizations who have done the most to promote world peace. It has been awarded since 1901. The award started after a famous Swedish scientist named Alfred Nobel died. He left lots of money in his will; it is now divided up and given out each year as the Nobel Peace Prize.

The prize often goes to one person or organization. In 2011, it went to three people. This is only the second time that three people have shared the award. In 2011, the Nobel Peace Prize went to Ellen Johnson Sirleaf, Leymah Gbowee, and Tawakkol Karman.

Ellen Johnson Sirleaf is the president of Liberia. Her goal is to bring peace and freedom to her country. She was chosen for the Peace Prize because of her hard work for women's rights. She hopes that girls around the world will see her as a role model.

Leymah Gbowee is also from Liberia and is a peace activist. She led a group in Liberia to fight for women to get the right to vote in elections. She also helped to end a civil war in her country. Gbowee got the Peace Prize for helping women to have more freedom and for keeping women safe.

The third winner, Tawakkol Karman, also won the prize for her work with women. She is the first Arab woman ever to win the Nobel Peace Prize. Her goal is to bring freedom and self-esteem to people in her country.

Conclusion
Tells how the article ends

These three women received their awards at a ceremony in Oslo, Norway. The Peace Prize ceremony is held in Oslo every year.

Note how the author of this piece:

- Named the article in the first paragraph, putting the article's title in quotation marks.

  If the author of this piece had been summarizing a book, she would need to italicize or underline the title.

  Alfred Nobel: A Biography, is a book by Kenne Fant. It tells interesting facts about the Swedish scientist who created the famous Nobel Peace Prize.

- Rewrote the article using her own words instead of copying from the article.

- Probably made the summary much shorter than the article.

Cause-and-Effect Essay

A **cause-and-effect essay** tells what happened and why it happened.

Parts of a Cause-and-Effect Essay

- An introduction that tells what the essay will explain
- One or more causes that tell why something happened
- Key facts that help explain the cause-and-effect relationship
- A conclusion that wraps up the essay and ties ideas together

Introduction
Tells the topic of the essay

When he was elected, Mayor Griggs said he would make the town shine. He sure kept his promise! In fact, he has been one of the best mayors this town has ever had. Want to know why? He feels the community can work to make the town better.

Causes tell why something happened.

First, he asked people to volunteer for projects around town. One group cleaned up trash in the parks and ball fields. Another worked to clean up school yards and playgrounds. A third cleaned up other public spaces, like the lawn in front of Town Hall. **Now** there is almost no litter anywhere in town.

Next, Mayor Griggs formed a group of volunteers to make the town prettier. This group planted trees and flowers and repaired a few of the crumbling buildings.

Effects tell what happened.

As a result, downtown looks beautiful! Main Street is lined with flowers, and the buildings have a new coat of paint.

Other Transitions
Due to
From that time
Therefore
Now
Then
For this reason

The mayor **also** started a program to persuade people to bring their old books to the public library. The library got so many books, they did not have space to put them all! In **addition**, he asked people to give food to the homeless shelter **so that** everyone who lives in our town can get enough to eat.

Then Mayor Griggs decided to do something about crime. He hired more police officers and encouraged neighbors to form neighborhood watch groups. **Because** he did, there has been much less crime, especially in the downtown area.

All in all, life is better in our town because of Mayor Griggs. Not only has life in town improved, but people are working together. **Because** of the mayor's work, there is a stronger sense of community. **More than that**, downtown looks beautiful. People who live in our town feel safe. This has become a wonderful place to live **since** Mayor Griggs was elected.

Note how the author of this piece:

- Introduced the topic of the essay.

  Other ways she could have introduced the essay include telling how the mayor made the town more beautiful or safer.

  The town has never been more beautiful than it has been since Mayor Griggs took office.

- Showed cause-and-effect relationships in paragraph 5:

  *He hired more police officers and encouraged neighbors to form neighborhood watch groups. **Because he did,** there has been much less crime, especially in the downtown area.*

Problem-Solution Composition

A **problem-solution composition** is an essay that presents a problem and offers several ways to solve it.

Parts of a Problem-Solution Composition

- An introduction that tells about the problem
- Body paragraphs that offer several solutions
- A conclusion that tells the best solution

Let's Stop Littering

Introduction
Presents the problem

Our school's neighbors are complaining about litter on their property. After school, kids walking home throw trash on the neighbors' lawns. This makes our school look bad. We have to prove to our neighbors that not only are we good kids, but we respect our neighborhood.

One way to solve the problem is to have trash cans by each exit door in the school. Students should put their trash in the cans before they walk home. We could have an all-school assembly to remind kids not to litter and to tell them about the trash can rule. When the last bell rings, volunteers could stand by the cans and remind students to use them.

Body
Has paragraphs that each offer one solution to the problem

Another solution to stop the littering is to ban students from taking home any lunch leftovers. Leftovers are the biggest litter problem. Neighbors complain that kids dump potato chip bags, juice boxes, and plastic bags with half-eaten sandwiches. Our school already tells kids

Other Transitions
The first way
The second way
Another way
The next solution
Finally
Lastly

to eat all of their lunch and not to throw food away. Not allowing students to take leftovers home might make kids eat all of their lunch. Maybe they would learn not to bring more lunch to school than they can eat.

The most excellent solution is to have clean up teams at our school. Every day, one class would spend recess or part of their lunch hour picking up litter in our neighbors' yards. A teacher could be there to supervise. If kids had to pick up the trash, they would be less likely to litter. Best of all, it would be a great way for students to meet our neighbors and show them that we are good kids who care about the neighborhood. With this solution, everybody wins!

For each solution, the writer uses language to persuade the audience.

Conclusion
Tells about the best solution

Note how the author of this piece:

- Clearly organized his solutions, putting the best one last.

  One way to solve the problem . . .

  Another solution to stop the littering . . .

  The most excellent solution . . .

- Used persuasive language.

  If kids had to pick up the trash, they would be less likely to litter.

  . . . it would be a great way for students to meet our neighbors . . .

  . . . everybody wins!

Compare-and-Contrast Essay

A **compare-and-contrast essay** tells how two or more things are alike and how they are different.

Parts of a Compare-and-Contrast Essay

- An introduction that tells what will be compared and contrasted
- Details that show how the topics are alike and different
- An organization that makes sense: similarities and differences, differences and then similarities, or differences and similarities point by point
- Transition words that show whether things are being compared or contrasted
- A conclusion that sums up the information

Introduction
Tells what will be compared and contrasted

Science museums and art museums are different in many ways, yet they share some similarities.

Transition words tell if the topics are compared or contrasted

Art museums display many kinds of art. This includes paintings, sculpture, costumes, and photography. These are objects made by people. **In contrast,** science museums show a lot of things found in nature. These could be things like bones, rocks, or dinosaur models.

Body
Gives details that tell how the topics are different

Visitors to art museums cannot touch the art. **However,** in science museums, visitors can often touch true-to-life things. Science museums can **also** have interactive exhibits where visitors can touch objects, watch videos, or play with computer programs.

Other Transitions
Like
Similarly
Unlike
Differently
Neither
To compare
To contrast
For example

Body
Gives details
that tell how
the topics are
similar

The art museum in our town is often very quiet. People walk through it slowly and examine the art silently. **By contrast**, the science museum is sometimes very loud. There are more kids who visit it each day. They talk as they play with the exhibits.

On the other hand, both museums have displays that show how people lived long ago. For example, the art museum shows Native American art, including costumes, tools, and jewelry. You can see some of these same kinds of things at the science museum in the rooms about how people used to live. Also, **both** museums can be great places to visit on a rainy day. Art and science museums are filled with things to explore. **Both** museums encourage you to learn in an exciting way. They are great places to visit on a school field trip or with your family.

Conclusion
Sums up the
information

Art museums and science museums are equally great places to visit. No matter which one you visit, you are sure to have an interesting experience!

Note how the author of this piece:

- Organized the essay with differences first and then similarities.

  Other ways he could have organized the essay include giving similarities first and then differences, or giving similarities and differences on the same topic within the same paragraph.

- Used transition words, such as:

  alike, different, in contrast, however, both

How-to Essay

A **how-to essay** explains how to complete a task. Clear, organized instructions tell readers exactly what to do.

Parts of a How-to Essay

- An introduction that tells readers what they will learn
- A body that explains each how-to step in order
- A conclusion that tells the result of completing all the steps

Beginning
Tells readers what they will learn

Examples
help readers understand.

Body
Shows all the how-to steps in order

How to Write a Song

Songs do not just happen by magic. Someone has to think up the words and write them down. Then the words have to be put to music. It is easy to write a song if you know how to do it.

First, write down some ideas. You could write a song about a family member or a friend. You could also make a song about a place you like. If you don't want to write about something real, then write about something make-believe. Maybe you could write about a super-hero, an alien, or even another world. Make a list of all your song ideas.

Second, decide which idea you want to use. Think about each song idea on your list. How does it make you feel? A song about your mom could be cuddly. A song about a brother or sister might be silly. A song about a super-hero might be a loud rock song. Write down your feelings for each song idea on your list. Then choose which idea you will make into a song.

Other Transitions
Before
During
Near
Under
After
Meanwhile
As soon as
Last

Third, write a poem about your idea. It can be a rhyming poem or free verse. It must be long enough to make into a song. Three or four stanzas or about half a page should be enough.

Next, make up a melody. Think about the way your poem makes you feel. This will help you create a melody. Sing the words out loud and try out different tunes. When you find one that you like, practice it over and over so you will not forget it.

Finally, it is time to share your song. Sing it for your family and friends. Teach them to sing it. If you like writing songs, think about starting a band with some friends and performing your songs.

Song writing is fun. If you follow all of these steps, you will see how easy it is. Who knows? Maybe someday you will be a famous songwriter.

Note how the author of this piece:

- Presents the steps in order and uses transition words to connect them.

First, you need to write down some ideas.

Second, you have to decide which idea you want to use.

Third, you should write a poem about your idea.

Next, you should make up a melody for your song.

Finally, it is time to share your song.

Explanation

An **explanation** is writing that explains something or tells how or why something happens. When you write an explanation, you provide readers with information about a specific topic.

Parts of an Explanation

- An introduction that gets readers interested in the topic
- A body that uses logical order to present facts and examples explaining the topic
- A conclusion that sums up the explanation in a meaningful way

Where Does Chocolate Come From?

Introduction
Gets readers' attention

The average person in the United States eats ten pounds of chocolate each year. That is a lot of chocolate and a lot of work for the people who make it. So how exactly is chocolate made?

Chocolate starts out as cocoa beans. The beans come from cacao trees that grow on farms in countries near the equator. Each tree makes lots of big, orange seedpods shaped like squash. The cocoa beans are inside the pods. Cocoa beans are the tree's seeds.

Body
Contains information presented in a logical way

First, workers harvest the ripe pods using large knives attached to poles. Then, they split the pods open and scoop out the insides. The cocoa beans are covered with pulp that smells sweet and lemony. After that, the workers put the beans in shallow boxes or in piles. Some of the pulp stays on the beans. Then the workers cover the

Other Transitions
When
Before
During
After a while
Meanwhile
Later
Last

beans with big banana leaves. After about a week in the sun, the pulp breaks down and the beans begin to taste like chocolate. Next, the workers put the beans on bamboo mats to dry. The beans are dried for several days. During this drying process, the beans lose most of their moisture and about half their weight. The dried beans are hard. They have a deep brown center, and they smell like chocolate. Now the workers load the cocoa beans into sacks. They put the sacks onto trucks, boats, and planes and send them to chocolate factories all around the world.

Finally, chocolate makers in the factories roast the beans and grind them up. The ground cocoa beans turn into a thick chocolate liquid. The liquid is made into solid unsweetened chocolate, cocoa butter, or cocoa powder. Other ingredients can be added to sweeten and flavor the chocolate.

Conclusion
Wraps up the topic in a meaningful way

It takes a lot of work to make cocoa beans into chocolate. But once you have chocolate, you can use it to make other things. Most of them are sweet, like cakes, candy, ice cream, and cookies. Unsweetened chocolate can also be mixed with spicy ingredients like onions, garlic, and chili peppers to make a special sauce for Mexican meals. However you use it, chocolate is one of the most delicious foods you will ever eat.

Science Observation Report

A **science observation report** tells what you learned from completing a science experiment.

Parts of a Science Observation Report

- The purpose of the experiment
- Your hypothesis
- The materials you need to do the experiment
- The procedure you followed
- Your observations during the experiment
- Your conclusions, or what you learned

Purpose
Tells what you plan to find out

Hypothesis
Tells what you think will happen

Materials
Tells what you need to do the experiment

Procedure
Tells step-by-step what you did

Does Temperature Affect Popcorn?

Purpose: To find out if the storage temperature of microwave popcorn affects how well it pops.

Hypothesis: I think popcorn will pop best if it is at room temperature.

Materials: 9 bags of microwave popcorn (same kind and same expiration date)
Kitchen counter
Refrigerator
Freezer
Microwave oven
Cookie sheet
A permanent marker, notebook, and pencil

Procedure:

1. I used the marker to label 3 popcorn bags "freezer," 3 "refrigerator," and 3 "room temperature."
2. Then I put the "freezer" bags in the freezer, the

Numbering the steps makes the procedure easy to follow.

"refrigerator" bags in the refrigerator, and the "room temperature" bags on the kitchen counter.

3. I waited 24 hours.

4. After that, I took one bag out of the freezer and popped it for 80 seconds.

5. Next, I spread the popcorn on the cookie sheet, counted the popped and unpopped kernels, and observed the way the popcorn looked. I recorded the information in my notebook.

6. Finally, I repeated this for each bag of popcorn.

Observations
Tells what you saw, or observed, while doing the experiment

Observations: The freezer popcorn was the best. The pieces looked bigger, and more of the kernels popped. The refrigerator and counter popcorn looked the same, but the refrigerator popcorn had less unpopped kernels than the counter popcorn.

Conclusion
Tells what you learned and whether your hypothesis was correct

Conclusion: My hypothesis was incorrect. Popcorn pops best when it is cold.

Note how the author of this piece:

• Recorded the results in a notebook.

• Included complete and accurate information.
  This writer might also have written in the notebook how many cups of popped corn each bag made.

• Compared and wrote data about each bag in each series (freezer, refrigerator, counter).

Research Report

A **research report** uses facts and details from outside sources to inform readers about a topic.

✏ Parts of a Research Report

- An introduction that tells the topic of the report
- A body with facts and details that support the main idea
- Information from outside sources like books, magazines, and the Internet
- A conclusion that sums up the main point

Introduction
Tells what the report will be about and interests the reader

Main Idea

Body
Includes facts and details that support the main idea

The Prehistoric Trackways: A Pathway into the Past

America has many places with historical and cultural value. Some places are so important that the government protects them by naming them national monuments. One of the newest national monuments is the Prehistoric Trackways National Monument near Las Cruces, New Mexico.

This national monument contains fossils that are more than 280-million years old. The World Museum of Natural History says that a scientist named Jerry MacDonald discovered the fossils. In 1987, he was hiking in the Robledo Mountains when he found fossilized animal tracks in the rocks. Since then, he has worked to uncover the fossils and find out about the animals that made them. His discovery turned out to be the world's most important collection of fossil tracks. They came from a time on Earth called the

Other Transitions
First
Next
After that
During
After a while
Meanwhile
Later
Last

Information
Source
Tells where
specific
information
was found

Permian Period. According to the New Mexico Bureau of Land Management, the monument contains fossils of amphibians, reptiles, insects, plants, and petrified wood.

There is a book about the monument called *Traces of a Permian Seacoast*. It says the Permian Period was 251 to 299 million years ago. Back then, all the Earth's continents were one big supercontinent called Pangea. New Mexico was near the equator. A shallow tropical sea covered its southern part. That is why some of the fossils in the Prehistoric Trackways National Monument are of sea animals like brachiopods.

Ancient animals that lived along the seacoast included different kinds of fish, insects, spiders, and scorpions. Amphibians, like snakes and salamanders, lived there, too. So did big predators like the ferocious sail-backed dimetrodon. Fossils from all of these animals can be found in the new monument. It also contains fossils of logs, trees, and other plants. Some of the plants were like those we see today. The Walchia plant probably looked like a modern Norfolk Pine tree.

Conclusion
Wraps up the
main points of
the report

Jerry MacDonald worried that hikers and all-terrain vehicles might destroy these valuable fossils. So, he asked the United States Government to protect them. In 2009, Congress agreed to make this area a national monument.

The Prehistoric Trackways National Monument is so new that there are no signs, hiking paths, or smooth roads. Work is underway for that to change. For now, people can hike, ride horses, or drive off-road vehicles to see certain parts of the monument. More of the fossils can be seen at the Jerry MacDonald Paleozoic Trackways collection in the New Mexico Museum of Natural History and Science.

Graphs, Diagrams, and Charts

Graphs, diagrams, and charts are helpful to show data and make comparisons. A report or summary can be made even better through the use of these types of graphic organizers.

Graphs and Charts
Are used to compare or show how something changes over time

Bar Graphs
Use vertical or horizontal bars to compare how many or how much

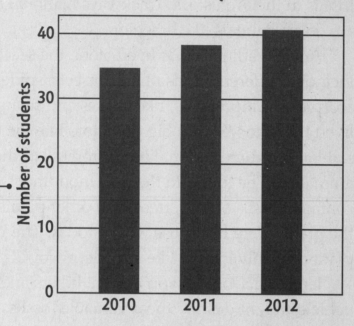

Fourth Graders in All-City Chorus 2010-2012

This bar graph compares how many fourth graders were in the All-City Chorus in the years 2010, 2011, and 2012.

Line Graphs
Use straight lines in a grid to show or compare how many or how much

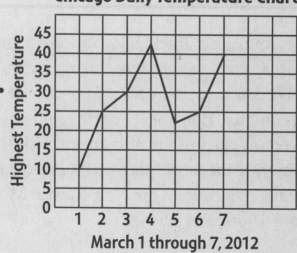

Chicago Daily Temperature Chart

Line graph showing the highest outside temperatures in Chicago for March 1-7, 2012

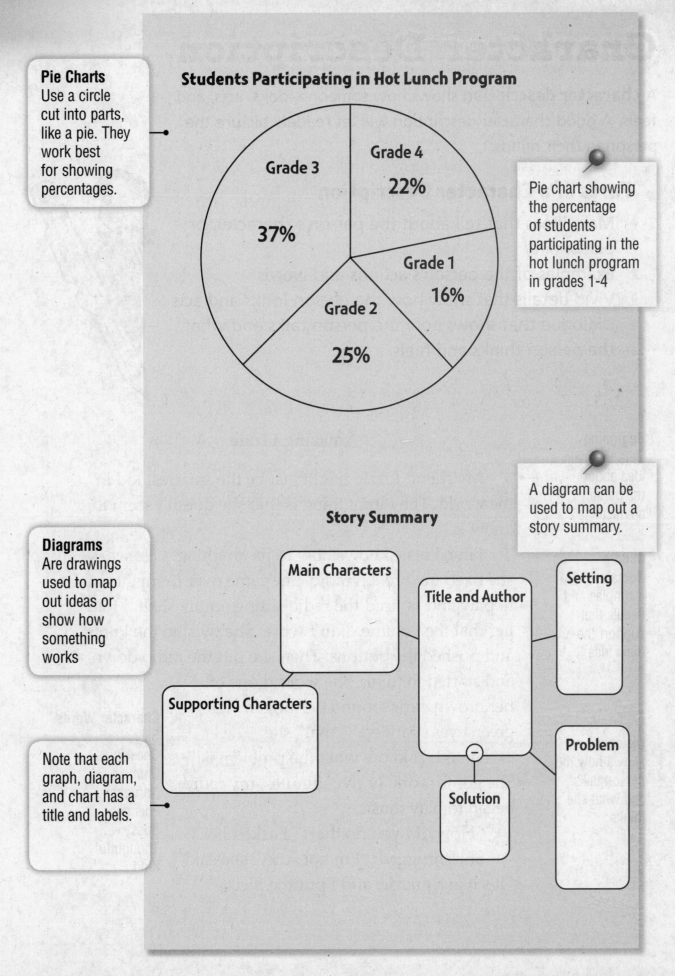

Pie Charts
Use a circle cut into parts, like a pie. They work best for showing percentages.

Students Participating in Hot Lunch Program

Grade 3
37%

Grade 4
22%

Grade 1
16%

Grade 2
25%

Pie chart showing the percentage of students participating in the hot lunch program in grades 1-4

A diagram can be used to map out a story summary.

Story Summary

Main Characters

Title and Author

Setting

Supporting Characters

Solution

Problem

Diagrams
Are drawings used to map out ideas or show how something works

Note that each graph, diagram, and chart has a title and labels.

Character Description

A **character description** shows how someone looks, acts, and feels. A good character description will let readers picture the person in their minds.

Parts of a Character Description

- Main ideas that tell about the person's character, or personality
- Examples of the person's actions and words
- Vivid details that show how the person looks and acts
- Dialogue that shows how the person talks and what the person thinks and feels

Beginning
Tells the main idea about the person's character

Middle
Contains examples and details that support the main idea

Dialogue shows how the person talks and what she thinks.

Amazing Lizzie

My friend Lizzie might just be the smartest kid in the world. The funny thing is that she doesn't seem to know it.

First, Lizzie knows how to fix anything. Last week, she fixed my broken radio. She came over to my house to play and noticed the radio sitting on my shelf. I told her that the volume didn't work. She twisted the knobs and pushed the buttons. Then she put the radio down and started to think. She wound one of her brown curls around her finger. Her green eyes sparkled. "Aha!" she exclaimed. "I know what the problem is!" She got to work. In five minutes, my radio began to play music.

"How did you do that?" I asked her.

She shrugged. "I'm not sure," she said. "It's like a puzzle, and I put the pieces

Character Words
Silly
Cheerful
Clumsy
Nervous
Friendly
Bossy
Thoughtful
Kind

together." This was the same answer I got when Lizzie fixed our computer printer, TV, and toaster.

Second, Lizzie knows something about everything. She can tell you how clouds are formed or how many different kinds of birds are found in Canada. Do you want to know how bridges are built? Just ask Lizzie. Sometimes she'll give a short answer, like she did with the radio. Other times, she gets excited and won't stop talking. One time I asked her how jelly beans are made. For the next twenty minutes, she told me all about jelly bean factories. Some people might think that this would be annoying. But Lizzie makes learning fun. She might even crack a good joke. "Hey, why did the jelly bean go to school?" she asked me. "Because he wanted to be a smartie!" Then she bent over and laughed her head off.

Lizzie never brags about being smart. She says that everyone knows something that other people don't. I guess she's right. But to me, Lizzie sure seems like a smartie in a world of jelly beans.

Vivid descriptions show how the person acts and feels.

Ending Reviews the main idea of the character description

Note how the authors of this piece:

- Described the person's appearance by mentioning her hair and eye color.

Other ways to describe how a person looks include telling about her age, clothing, or unique physical features.

No one believes that Lizzie is only nine because she is so tall.

Lizzie always wears shorts and sneakers.

Lizzie has freckles across her nose and a dimple on her right cheek.

Personal Narrative

A **personal narrative** tells about an interesting or important event in the writer's life. A personal narrative about the writer's life may also be called an autobiography.

Parts of a Personal Narrative

- A beginning that grabs readers' attention and makes them want to read more
- True events told in time order
- Vivid descriptions of the people and events in the narrative
- A first-person point of view
- An ending that wraps up the narrative or tells how the writer felt

A Race to Remember

Beginning
Pulls readers into the story

"Will I really be able to do this?" I wondered to myself. I had spent the last month getting ready to swim this race. But I still didn't feel like I could do it. I would have to swim 100 yards. That's four full laps across the pool! To make things worse, I would be swimming against Rosalie again. I had never beaten Rosalie in a race, and there was nothing I wanted more.

Middle
Tells about the events in the order that they happened

I walked up to my starting block at the edge of the pool. Rosalie was already standing on her block in the lane to my left. Oh no! We would be swimming right next to each other! Rosalie smiled and waved. Butterflies filled my stomach. I gave her a little wave back. Then I put my

Other Transitions
First
Next
After that
During
After a while
Meanwhile
Later
Last

goggles over my eyes and got ready to dive into the pool.

"Swimmers, on your mark," the starter announced. I bent over until the tips of my fingers touched the block. Beep! The buzzer sounded. The race was on! I dove into the cold water and swam as fast as I could. I saw Rosalie every time I took a breath. She was already ahead of me. I pulled my arms through the water as hard as I could. I kicked with all my might. By the start of the second lap, we were neck-in-neck.

That's when things got really hard. My body became tired quickly, and had a hard time catching my breath. My legs and arms began to cramp. I didn't know anymore if Rosalie was in front of me or behind me. Would I make it? I knew that I had to keep going. I made the turn at the end of the third lap. Only one more lap to go.

Now I could hear the crowd cheering. This gave me the extra push I needed. I swam harder than I ever had before. Finally, my hand slapped against the wall. The long race was over.

When I lifted my head out of the water, I saw Rosalie. She was looking at the scoreboard at the end of the pool. It showed that she had won the race. The funny thing is that I didn't really care. In a way, I had won, too. I not only made it through the race, but I also beat my best lap time. I had never felt so proud. This sure was a race to remember!

Biography

A **biography** is a true story that tells about the main events in a person's life. It explains why the person is special or interesting, or how he or she made a difference.

✏ Parts of a Biography

- A beginning that introduces the person to readers
- A middle with interesting facts and details about the person
- Events told in time order, or sequence
- An ending that wraps up the biography or gives a final thought

Beginning
Tells why the person is important or interesting

Middle
Tells interesting facts and details in time order

Matthew Henson: Arctic Explorer

Matthew Henson stood on the icy snow. It had taken 20 years, but he was finally "on top of the world." Henson was the first person to reach the North Pole. He became known as one of the world's greatest explorers.

Matthew Henson was born to African-American parents in Baltimore, Maryland, in 1866. Both of his parents died before he turned 13. Henson was alone in the world. He slept on the floor of the restaurant where he worked. Then, in 1879, his life changed. A sea captain hired Henson to work on his ship. Henson spent his teenage years learning how to read maps and sail ships.

In 1887, Henson met an explorer named Robert Peary. Peary hired Henson to go with him to Nicaragua and draw maps of the jungle there. The men traveled through Central America for the next

Other Transitions
First
Next
After that
During
After a while
Meanwhile
Later
Last

two years. When the trip ended, Peary decided to go after his real dream. He wanted to be the first person in the world to reach the North Pole. He asked Henson to go with him.

Between 1891 and 1908, Peary and Henson tried to reach the North Pole four times. Each time, they started from base camps in Greenland or Canada. Then they traveled north. The trips were very dangerous. The weather was extremely cold and windy. The men also had trouble finding food. Henson became stronger, though. He made friends with the Eskimo and learned a lot from them. He learned how to break trails, hunt for food, and make clothing from animal fur. Henson even learned how to build sleds and run a dog team. These skills helped the men survive.

In April 1909, Peary and Henson tried one last time to reach the North Pole. The men didn't have a lot of supplies and could make only one trip. Henson ran the lead sled and moved quickly. In five days, Henson traveled over 200 miles. He reached the North Pole shortly before Peary did. Henson became the first person to reach what is known as the top of the world.

Unfortunately, Henson didn't have a lot of time to celebrate. People didn't believe that he and Peary really reached the North Pole. They had to prove that they were telling the truth. Then, Peary took all the credit. He said that he was the first one to reach the North Pole.

Finally, in 1937, people learned the truth. Henson received many awards after that, including the Congressional Medal of Honor. He even had schools and a ship named after him. Matthew Henson died in 1955. He is still remembered as one of the world's greatest explorers.

Keep readers interested with stories about what the person experienced.

Ending
Wraps up the biography and gives a final thought

Fictional Narrative

A **fictional narrative** is a made-up story about characters who solve a problem.

Parts of a Fictional Narrative

- A plot with a problem or mystery to be solved
- One or more characters that work to try to solve the problem
- Details about what the characters look like and where the story takes place
- An ending that tells how the characters solve the problem

Beginning
Introduces the characters, setting, and problem

Mystery Under the School

A new gym was being built at school, and Mrs. Arnold's class went to see the construction site. They walked around and watched the workers digging up the ground to lay the foundation. While she looked around, Sarah noticed something shiny on the ground. It was a coin, but it didn't look like any coin she'd ever seen before. Rob also spotted something metal on the ground and, after some digging, he found a beat-up metal pot.

The plot has a mysterious event or problem to be solved.

"What do you think these are?" Rob asked.

"I don't know," said Sarah. "Let's see if someone who works here left them behind."

Sarah and Rob showed the coin and pot to the construction foreman. He said they couldn't belong to any of the workers—no one was allowed to bring metal to the site because of the machines they used. Sarah and Rob were stumped, but they decided they wanted to find out more.

Other Transitions
First
Next
After that
During
After a while
Meanwhile
Later
Last

Details show clues about the mystery and how the characters solve it.

Middle
Includes details about how the characters solve the problem

Ending
Shows how the characters solved the mystery

"Why don't you guys do a little bit of research on the town?" suggested Mrs. Arnold.

Sarah went to the library and found a book about old coins. The book a had a photo of a coin from 1817 that looked just like the one she'd found. She learned that the coins were used by some of the first people who moved to the town.

Rob went to the town historical society. He showed the pot to a historian who knew a lot about the area. The historian said, "There was once a fort on the same site as the school. Many of the first settlers in our town lived there."

Sarah and Rob compared what they found and agreed that coin and the pot were pretty neat. "I can't believe we touched something so old!" said Rob.

"How exciting!" said Mrs. Arnold when Sarah and Rob shared what they had found. "Who knew there was so much history under our school?"

Note how the author of this piece:

- Introduced the story to show the characters and the problem.

  Other ways she could have introduced the story include hooking the reader in with an interesting event.

  Sarah saw something shiny on the ground, and it turned out to be something unexpected: an old coin unlike one she had ever seen before!

- Used details to show how Rob and Sarah worked out the mystery:

  Sarah went to the library and found a book about coins.
  Rob went to the town historical society.

Play

A **play** is a story performed by actors in front of an audience. The scenes, dialogue, and characters' actions tell the entire story.

Parts of a Play

- Descriptions of the characters and setting
- Lines of dialogue that tell what the actors say
- Stage directions that tell what the actors do or how they should say their lines
- Props, or objects that make the scene more realistic

> Setting tells where and when the play takes place.

SCENE ONE (*A dark night on a country road in 1776. A British soldier blocks the road, stage right. Two American boys, ten years old, enter stage left. They hide behind a tree.*)

TOM: (*whispers*) If we're going to get this note to General Washington, we have to get it past the guard. That won't be easy.

> Dialogue tells what characters say

JAMES: (*whispers*) Yeah, he looks tough. How will we get around him?

TOM: (*whispers*) I don't know.

JAMES: (*whispers*) We'll have to trick him. I'll get him to look in the other direction and you sneak by.

TOM: That's a good plan! Just be careful!

Other Words That Tell How to Say Lines

Shouts
Gasps
Angrily
Happily
Laughs
Sighs
Cries

JAMES: *(screams, runs toward guard)* Hey, you!

Props

GUARD: *(raises his gun)* Stop! Who goes there?

JAMES: Don't shoot! Oh, help me, sir! I'm being chased by a terrible monster, sir! He's got great big fangs and horrible red eyes. He says he is hungry for an English soldier.

GUARD: *(laughing)* Oh, goodness! Hungry for an English soldier, you say? Oh, my. Where is he?

JAMES: *(points at audience)* There he is!

Stage directions give actors instructions

Guard turns to look. Tom tiptoes behind him, exits. James takes off running after Tom.

Note how the author of this piece:

- Made the dialogue sound like real speech.

  That's a good plan! Be careful!

  Oh, goodness! Hungry for an English soldier, you say? Oh, my.

- Used props and stage directions to set the scene.

  Examples: The characters hide behind a tree. The guard has a gun. The characters whisper and laugh and run across the stage.

Tall Tale

A **tall tale** is a story about heroes who are larger than life.
They do things that no real person would do.

Parts of a Tall Tale

- A main character, or hero, who is bigger or stronger than a real person
- A problem that is solved by the hero in a funny or unbelievable way
- Might be based on a person from history who has been made to seem super strong or super big

Beginning
Introduces the story and tells the problem

Middle
Tells how the hero solves a problem

Ending
Shows how the hero solved the problem

Paul Bunyan Crosses the Ocean

One time, Paul Bunyan and his human-sized friends headed toward the ocean. They needed to cross to the other side so that they could bring supplies to their friends on another continent. When they got to the coast, there was not a boat in sight. They waited for ten days and ten nights. Still, not one boat came their way.

Paul wanted to help. He looked around but didn't see anything they could use for a boat. Then he looked at his two huge feet and had an idea. He took off his shoes and loaded half his friends into the right shoe and the other half into the left. He shoved them off into the water with a big heave-ho. He swam beside them to make sure his shoes did not tip over.

Finally, they arrived at the opposite shore. Everyone made it there safely, and none of the supplies had fallen into the water. Paul Bunyan saved the day!

Other Transitions
At first
Next
Then
After a while
Meanwhile
In the end
Later Last

Myth

A **myth** is a made-up story that explains why something happens or how something came to be. The characters in a myth are usually gods, goddesses, monsters, and heroes who have special powers or skills.

Parts of a Myth

- A beginning that introduces the characters and setting
- Natural events and strange characters
- A problem or conflict
- An ending that explains how the problem is solved

Beginning
Introduces the setting and characters

Long ago, a young woman named Arachne lived in a small village in Greece. People said that Arachne was so skilled at weaving that she must have been trained by the goddess Athena. Arachne didn't like hearing this. She said that Athena could not weave as well as she did. This made Athena angry. She visited Arachne and

The characters have a problem or conflict.

challenged her to a weaving contest. Arachne accepted.

For weeks, Arachne and Athena worked hard. Still, Arachne said that her work was far better than the goddess's. Athena could not stand Arachne's bragging one minute longer. "You silly, hateful girl!" screamed Athena. "If you love to weave so much, I will make it so you can weave forever!" With that, Athena turned Arachne into a spider.

Other Transitions
First
Next
After that
During
After a while
Meanwhile
Later
Last

Now, Arachne and all of her descendants would have to spin webs

Ending
Tells how the problem is solved

until the end of time. And that is how spiders came to be.

Opinion Essay

An **opinion essay** tells what the writer thinks about an issue or topic. The writer also gives strong reasons for the opinion.

Parts of an Opinion Essay

- An introduction that states the opinion
- Strong reasons that support the opinion
- Details and examples that support the reasons
- A conclusion that repeats the opinion in a new way

Introduction
States the writer's opinion

Reasons tell why the writer feels the way he or she does about a topic.

Body
Gives facts and opinions that explain and support the reasons

Harvest Carnival

I really love that my school has so many fun events. We have a winter concert and a student art show. We also have a sports day every spring. But the best school event is the Harvest Carnival.

To start with, the Harvest Carnival has great decorations. Red, orange, and yellow ribbons cover the walls and doorways. The jungle gym gets covered in big bunches of black and gold balloons. Teachers and parents put bales of hay and pumpkins all over the schoolyard. There are also scarecrows wearing funny clothes and hats. All these decorations make people excited about the fall season.

There is also a lot of yummy food at the Harvest Carnival. Parents and teachers cook hot dogs, chicken, and vegetables on a huge outdoor grill. These meals are always hot and delicious. But, if your belly isn't full, there's even more to enjoy! There are bags of popcorn and roasted pumpkin seeds. Last year, we even had a

Other Transitions
First
Next
Then
One reason
The second reason
After that
During
Later
Finally

Strong descriptions convince readers to agree with the opinion.

big table with bowls of fruit, pies, and other treats. Of course, caramel apples are my favorite food to eat at the Harvest Carnival. Some of them are plain with only caramel. Others are covered in chocolate chips or peanuts.

Last, the Harvest Carnival has a lot of really fun games. In one game, you try to throw a ping-pong ball into a goldfish bowl. If you do it, you get to bring the goldfish home. In another game, you can win a prize by running with an egg in a spoon without dropping it. There is even a cake walk and a pie-eating contest. I spend all afternoon playing the games at the Harvest Carnival, and I still don't want to leave at the end of the day.

Conclusion Repeats the focus statement in a new way

My school has a lot of great events throughout the year. But nothing beats the Harvest Carnival. After all, where else can you see beautiful decorations, eat yummy food, and play exciting games?

Note how the author of this piece:

- Gave a reason in the topic sentence of each paragraph.

  To start with, the Harvest Carnival has great decorations.
  There is also a lot of yummy food at the Harvest Carnival.
  Last, the Harvest Carnival has a lot of really fun games.

- Used strong language and descriptions to convince readers that her reasons make sense.

  Red, orange, and yellow ribbons cover the walls and doorways.
  All these decorations **make people excited** about the fall season.
  These meals are always **hot** and **delicious.**

Persuasive Essay

A **persuasive essay** tells about a writer's opinion of a topic or issue. The writer gives reasons for the opinion and tries to convince readers to act or think in a certain way.

Parts of a Persuasive Essay

- An introduction that tells the writer's opinion and goal
- Reasons that support the writer's opinion
- Details, facts, or examples that explain each reason
- A conclusion that sums up the writer's goal and reasons

Introduction
Tells the writer's opinion and goal

Reasons support the opinion.

Notice how the writer answers questions or concerns that readers may have.

Recess!

Students at our school get two recesses each day. There is a 15 minute recess in the morning. Then there is a 20 minute lunch recess. This is not enough time for kids to run and play. The school should add another recess to the school day.

First of all, students are in school for almost seven hours each day. That's a long time! Think about it. Would an adult like sitting at a desk for seven hours with only 35 minutes off? Of course not! And it's even harder for kids. We have lots of energy and need to move around. Some people might say that P.E. gives students extra time to move and play. However, this isn't really true. My school doesn't have P.E. every day. Also, P.E. is still a class. It's not a recess.

Second, adding another recess to the school day will help keep kids healthy.

Other Transitions
To start with
Then
In addition
Next
As well as
For example
Later
Finally

Details, facts, and examples explain or support the reasons.

The strongest reason usually goes last.

Conclusion
Sums up the writer's goal and reasons

Kids play basketball and soccer during recess. They also play tag and climb on the jungle gym. These are all great forms of exercise. Exercise is an important part of staying fit. The best part is that kids don't think of recess time as exercise time. They just think they're having fun.

Last, having an extra recess will help students in the classroom. I know that I have a hard time thinking when I've been in the classroom too long. Some kids also get rowdy. They start talking to friends. They move around in their seats. This isn't good for the teachers or the students. However, kids might act better if they had another recess. It would give them a chance to get their energy out. Then they would be able to concentrate better and focus on their school work.

Our school should add an extra recess to the school day. It will give kids a break they need. It will help to keep them healthy. Finally, it will help them in the classroom. Don't you think that these things are just as important as math and reading? I sure do!

Note how the author of this piece:

- Gives details and examples that explain and support her reasons. Another way she can support her reasons is to add facts and quotes.

  Nine out of 10 students say they don't get enough recess time.
  Mr. Martin, one of the fourth grade teachers, said, "Kids seem to work a lot harder inside when they have more time to play outside."

- Uses strong language to convince her readers.

  Would an adult like sitting at a desk for seven hours with only 35 minutes off? Of course not!

Response to Literature: Play

A **response to a play** tells about a play that you have read or seen and what you think about it.

✏ Parts of a Response to a Play

- An introduction that states an opinion about the play
- Reasons that explain the opinion
- Details and examples from the play that support the reasons
- A conclusion that sums up the response

Introduction
States the title of the play and the writer's opinion

Body
Has reasons that support the writer's opinion

Annie

The musical play <u>Annie</u> tells about an 11-year-old orphan named Annie. Annie has had a hard life. Her parents left her at the orphanage when she was only a baby. To make things worse, the orphanage director, Miss Hannigan, is a very mean woman. None of this gets Annie down, though. She always shows what a smart and kind person she is.

First, Annie comes up with a smart plan to escape from the orphanage. She waits for Mr. Bundles to pick up the laundry. Then, while he is talking to Miss Hannigan, Annie jumps in the laundry basket and covers herself with blankets. Mr. Bundles leaves the orphanage. He doesn't know that he's also leaving with Annie. She tricks both Mr. Bundles and Miss Hannigan.

Second, Annie shows how kind and smart she is when she meets a stray dog. Annie sees the dog right after she escapes

Other Transitions
In addition
Next
After that
During
After a while
Meanwhile
Later
Finally

Details and examples explain the reasons

from the orphanage. The dog looks scared and sad, so Annie hugs him and sings to him. She even names him Sandy. Then a dog catcher comes to take Sandy away. Annie comes up with another smart trick. She tells the dog catcher that Sandy is hers. The dog catcher believes her and leaves Sandy alone.

Last, Annie is very smart and kind with Mr. Warbucks. At first, Mr. Warbucks seems like a grumpy, angry person. However, Annie knows better. She can tell that Mr. Warbucks is really sad and lonely. Annie does what she can to make Mr. Warbucks happy. She talks to him, sings with him, and makes him laugh. Mr. Warbucks soon feels joyful again. In fact, Annie's kindness makes Mr. Warbucks feel so happy that he decides to adopt her.

Conclusion Restates the author's opinion

Annie is a great play! Anyone who sees it will love how smart and kind Annie is. I know I sure did!

Note how the author of this piece:

- Wrote about a character in the play.

   Other good topics for a response essay include:

   An opinion about the plot: Is the play slow? Is the action exciting?

   An opinion about one or more settings in the play: Did the setting add to the drama? Did it create a happy or scary mood?

- Used specific details from the play to support her opinion.

   Annie jumps in the laundry basket and covers herself with blankets. The dog looks scared and sad, so Annie hugs him and sings to him.

Response to Poetry

A **response to poetry** explains a writer's reactions to a poem.

Parts of a Response to Poetry

- An introduction that states the writer's opinion
- Examples from the poem that explain the opinion
- A conclusion that sums up the ideas

Lights Along Main Street

I walked along an average street
And noticed all the lights
Placed above the cold concrete
To brighten dark fall nights.

The lights were not yet switched on.
(It was barely after three!)
So I stopped and gazed upon
Sights only I could see—

A rainy night, all things damp,
A sky with clouds and grey.
And overhead, the first bright lamp,
Lighting up my way.

In the distance, more and more,
Lanterns, lamps, and lights.
An evening at first dark and bored
Now is fully bright.

People strolling, busy crowds,
The smell of cinnamon treats,
Music from a theater, loud,
Light up my mind's Main Street.

Lights Along Main Street

Introduction
Introduces the poem, setting, and meaning

The poem "Lights Along Main Street" tells the story of a person walking along a street. The person is walking during the day. She notices the streetlights, even though they aren't on. She imagines what the lights will look like when it is nighttime. The person walking has a great imagination. She pictures a whole scene that isn't there, filling the poem with vivid images and descriptions.

Details show clues about the poem's meaning.

At the start of the poem, the author is walking along a street. She says it is "an average street." The poem's title names the street Main Street. I think she uses the words "average" and "main" so the poem could take place anywhere. It's also important that she's walking on an average street because later on, her imagination makes the street special.

Then, the author says it's "barely after three." This means it is daytime, and the lights aren't on yet. She wants to know what they look like, so she imagines. She says, "So I stopped and gazed upon / Sights only I could see—." Only she can see these sights because she is imagining them. At this point, I was so curious! She

Other Transitions
First
Next
After that
During
After a while
Meanwhile
Later
Last

could have imagined anything. She could have imagined a busy street with people walking and having fun. Instead, she imagines something very dark.

Indeed, she sees, "A rainy night, all things damp / A sky with clouds and grey." The author pictures a dark evening with rain. "All things damp" means that it has been raining for a long time. When it rains for a while, everything gets a little wet. **Further**, the author sees "clouds and grey." This sounds like the kind of night when you don't even want to go outside because it is so wet and rainy.

Next, the author sees "the first bright lamp." Here, I picture this dark scene where everything is sad and quiet. Then, out of the dim street scene, a light! The lamp is so bright that it stands out against the darkness. She says it is "lighting up my way." Now, she can see in front of her. Instead of seeing just the grey sky, the author can see the street. At first, she just sees more and more light. This means the street looks brighter.

Finally, in the light, everything looks happy. She sees people walking and gathering in a store. She also smells cinnamon and hears music. These lines are so important because these are the first people, smells, and sounds in the poem. Before, when it was dark outside, the poem was dark and empty. Now, when the lights are on, the poem is filled with people and things to smell and hear.

> **Body**
> Digs in further to find meaning in the poem

> More details help to discuss the poem's meaning.

The last line is: "Light up my mind's Main Street." I like that the author says it is her mind's street, and not just any street. This is not "an average street" or even "Main Street" anymore. This shows that the author now loves the street. It is no longer dark and dreary outside. Now it is bright and full of music. All of this is in her imagination, so I think she is really happy.

When I finished reading the poem, I looked back at the title: "Lights Along Main Street." I noticed that the focus of the title isn't darkness or rain. The focus is on light. The author never gets to see the lights turn on. However, she imagines what it would look like. Her imagination is so bright and full. I believe this is what the poem is about—finding excitement and happiness in dark places.

Conclusion
Sums up the main idea of the poem

Note how the author of this piece:

- Ends the response by going back to the beginning (the title).

  The author also could have ended the piece by talking about something general in the poem:

  I notice that the ideas of light and dark come up again and again in the poem.

- Shows what the poem did not say, but could have:

  She could have imagined a busy street with people walking and having fun.

Author Response

An **author response** is an essay that explains thoughts and opinions about an author's work or style of writing. It discusses two or more pieces written by the same author.

✏ Parts of an Author Response

- An introduction that states an opinion about the author
- Reasons that explain the opinion
- Details and examples from the author's work
- A conclusion that sums up the response

Introduction
States an opinion about the author's work

Body
Gives reasons that support the opinion

Roald Dahl

Have you ever read a book by Roald Dahl? If not, you should! Roald Dahl is a really great author. He writes exciting stories in which many funny and strange things happen.

A lot of funny and strange things happen in Roald Dahl's book, <u>James and the Giant Peach</u>. To start, a boy named James crawls inside a peach that is as big as a house. Seven insects live inside the peach. They are all as big as James and they talk! The giant peach rolls into the ocean with James and his insect friends inside. Seagulls carry the peach high into the sky. Then, an army of angry cloud men throw hail stones at the peach. At the end, the peach gets stuck on the Empire State Building in New York City. This book tells a very funny and strange story!

Other Transitions
First
Second
In addition
Next
After that
During
After a while
Meanwhile
Later
Finally

Details and examples explain the reasons.

Dahl's book <u>The Big Friendly Giant</u> also tells a funny, unusual story. In this book, giants blow dreams into kids' bedrooms. One nice giant takes a girl named Sophie to his home in Giant Country. The big friendly giant and Sophie ask the Queen of England to help them capture the mean giants. She sends an army to tie up the giants and throw them in a big pit. Of course, none of these things would happen in real life. They are just a part of the strange world of Roald Dahl.

<u>Matilda</u> is another one of Dahl's books that tells a funny and strange story. In this book, a five-year-old girl named Matilda has special powers. She can move things just by looking at them. One time, Matilda makes a piece of chalk lift into the air and write messages on the chalkboard. This scares the mean principal, Mrs. Trunchbull, and she runs away forever.

Conclusion Restates the opinion of the author

Roald Dahl is my favorite author. I love all the funny and strange things in his stories. He has a great imagination. Maybe you should try reading his books, too!

Note how the writer of this piece:

Wrote topic sentences that supported her opinion of the author's work.

A lot of funny and strange things happen in Roald Dahl's book, <u>James and the Giant Peach</u>.

Dahl's book <u>The Big Friendly Giant</u> also tells a funny, unusual story.

<u>Matilda</u> is another one of Dahl's books that tells a funny and strange story.

Book Review/Report

A **book review or report** tells about a book that you've read.
It gives a summary of the main ideas or events, the setting, and
the characters.

Parts of a Book Report

- An introduction that tells basic information about the
  book, including its title, author, and main idea
- A body that tells about the most important parts of
  the book
- A conclusion that sums up the report

Introduction
States the title,
author, and
main idea

The Lightning Thief by Rick Riordan is the first
book of the *Percy Jackson and the Olympians* series. It is a
fictional story that tells about the adventures of 12-year-
old Perseus Jackson. Percy is not like other boys,
though. He is the son of the Greek god Poseidon. In this
book, Percy must find a stolen lightning bolt. If he
doesn't find the bolt in time, the gods will go to war.

Body
Tells about the
most important
parts of the
book in time
order

Percy has a lot of problems in the beginning of the
book. He doesn't get along with his stepdad, and he
gets into a lot of trouble at school. Percy also can't
understand why so many strange things happen to him.
He is surprised when people turn into
monsters and attack him. Soon, Percy
learns the truth. He finds out that he is
half-human and half-god. He is sent to
Camp Half-Blood to keep him safe.

Percy learns a lot at Camp Half-Blood.
His teacher, Chiron, tells him that he is the
son of Poseidon, the Greek god of the sea.
Percy also learns that the god Zeus thinks

Other Transitions
First
Next
After that
During
After a while
Meanwhile
Later
Last

These paragraphs give more information about the main characters and events.

that Poseidon stole his lightning bolt. If the bolt is not returned in 14 days, Zeus will go to war against Poseidon. Percy is given a quest. He must go to the Underworld, find the bolt, and return it to Zeus on Mount Olympus before the 14 days have passed. Percy takes two friends on the quest to help him. He takes Grover, a satyr, and Annabeth, the daughter of Athena.

Percy, Grover, and Annabeth must travel from New York to Los Angeles to get to the Underworld. The trip is hard. The friends battle monsters along the way. Ares, the god of war, plays a lot of tricks on them. Luckily, Percy has a special shield that keeps him safe.

Things don't get any easier for Percy when he finally gets to the Underworld. Hades, the god of the Underworld, says he doesn't have the bolt. Hades also says that his helm of darkness is missing. He accuses Percy of stealing both. To prove it, Hades says that the lightning bolt is in Percy's back pack. And it is! Percy, Grover, and Annabeth escape the Underworld and go back to New York.

At the end of the book, Percy goes to Mount Olympus on the 600th floor of the Empire State Building. He gives the lightning bolt to Zeus. He also meets his dad for the first time. Percy then tells the gods that he thinks the god Kronos caused all of the trouble. Kronos ruled before Zeus did. Now he wants to bring down the Greek gods. Percy leaves Mount Olympus at the end of the meeting. Everyone kneels and calls him a hero. Finally, Percy goes home to be with his mother.

Conclusion Restates the title and author, and gives an opinion of the book

The Lightning Thief by Rick Riordan is an exciting, action-packed book. But, it's only the beginning of Percy Jackson's story. I can't wait to read the rest of the books in the series to find out what happens next!

Personal Narrative

A **personal narrative** describes an interesting or important event in the writer's life. It tells how the writer feels about the event.

Parts of a Personal Narrative

- A beginning that grabs readers' attention and makes them want to read more
- True events told in time order
- Vivid descriptions of the people and events in the narrative
- A first person point of view
- An ending that wraps up the narrative or tells how the writer felt

Beginning
Makes people want to read more

Last week, I had the best day in my life. I had my dad all to myself! This doesn't happen very often. My dad works a lot. When he gets home, he usually has to help my mom with my younger brother and sisters. Last Saturday, though, it was just my dad and me.

First, my dad woke me up early. We rode our bikes down to my favorite restaurant to have breakfast. I ate a plate full of waffles and drank a big cup of hot chocolate. Normally, meal time with my

Middle
Tells about the events in the order that they happened

family is kind of crazy. My younger sister always spills things, and everyone seems to talk at once. Not this time. I really enjoyed sitting at the table and talking with my dad. He told me funny stories about when he was my age. I told him about my teachers and friends.

Other Transitions
To start
Next
After that
During
After a while
Meanwhile
Later
Last

Vivid descriptions show what the writer is seeing, hearing, or feeling.

Interesting details show what is happening or what the writer is feeling.

Ending Tells how the story works out and how the writer feels

After breakfast, my dad and I drove into the city for a baseball game. We had seats right behind the third base line. We were so close that I could see the players' faces. I even came close to catching a foul ball! It was a really exciting game, too. Three players made home runs, and the score was tied at the end of the last inning. That's when the crowd really went wild. They cheered, clapped, and yelled until the last minute. Of course, my dad and I joined in the fun. We cheered so loudly that both of our voices eventually sounded like frogs. The game lasted a long time, but I didn't mind. I think I could have stayed there all day.

We got home in the late afternoon. My mom had gone shopping with my brother and sisters, so the house was very quiet. My dad and I made the most of the empty house. We sat on the couch, watched a movie, and ate popcorn. I couldn't think of a better way to end the best day ever. I just hope that I get another day with my dad soon!

Note how the author of this piece:

- Wrote an introduction that grabbed readers' attention.

  Other ways he could have introduced the narrative include asking a question or jumping into the action.

  Have you ever had a day that you were sure you would never forget?

  I pedaled my bike as fast as I could with my dad only a few feet behind me.

Labels and Captions

Labels and captions are words that describe graphs, diagrams, and charts. A label is a word or phrase. A caption is a sentence.

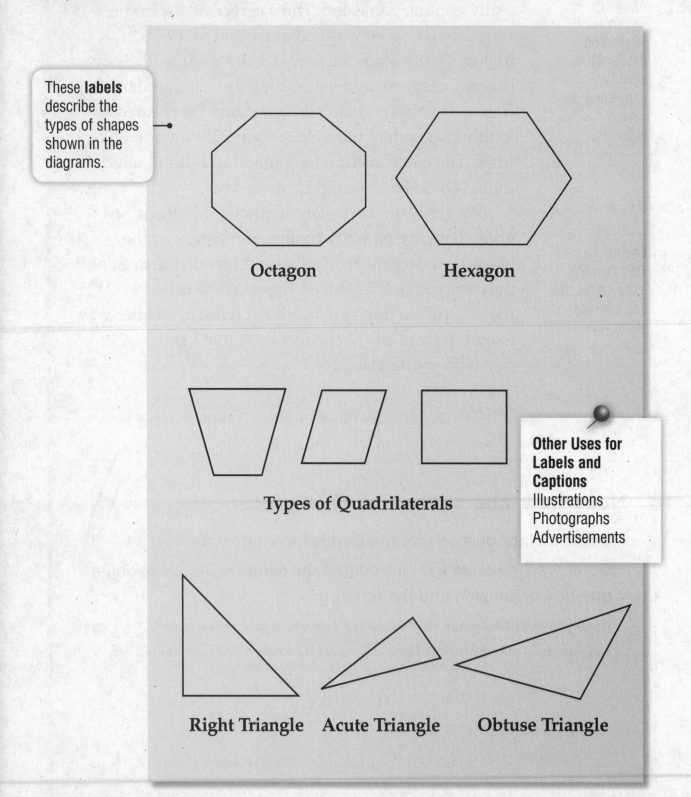

These **labels** describe the types of shapes shown in the diagrams.

Octagon   Hexagon

Types of Quadrilaterals

Other Uses for Labels and Captions
Illustrations
Photographs
Advertisements

Right Triangle   Acute Triangle   Obtuse Triangle

Students Participating in the Science Fair

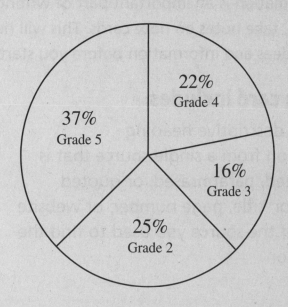

22%
Grade 4

37%
Grade 5

16%
Grade 3

25%
Grade 2

Adams Middle School held its 10th Annual Science Fair from March 15-19th. Though Grade 5 had the most participants, Grade 4 had the most winning projects.

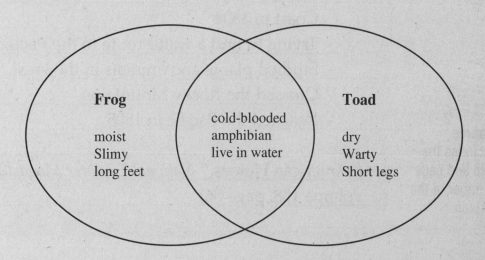

Frog

moist
Slimy
long feet

cold-blooded
amphibian
live in water

Toad

dry
Warty
Short legs

Frogs and toads belong to the same animal group, so they share similar traits. Even though they look alike at first glance, if you look carefully, you will notice differences in their appearance.

Notetaking Strategies

Gathering information is an important part of writing a report. As you research, take notes on note cards. This will help you organize your ideas and information before you start writing.

Each note card includes:

- A simple, descriptive heading
- Information from a single source that is summarized, paraphrased, or quoted
- The author, title, page number, or website address of the source you used to find the information

This information is summarized from a single source.

Meriwether Lewis and William Clark, Explorations

- Led expedition from the Missouri River to the Pacific Coast in 1804
- Trying to find a water route to the Pacific
- Studied plants and animals in the West
- Crossed the Rocky Mountains
- Reached the Pacific in 1805

Source
Includes the title and page number of the source

("American Heroes," *National Explorer Magazine*, volume 138, page 56)

William Clark

In charge of charting the course and making maps; drew some of the first maps of the Rocky Mountain region.

(Betty Newell, <u>The Life of William Clark</u>, page 264)

Meriwether Lewis

- Lewis spent a lot of time off the boat
- Studied the plants, animals, and rock formations that he saw along the way
- Filled dozens of books with drawings and diagrams

(http://www.---.edu/mlewis)

Lewis and Clark Expedition - Effect

"The Lewis and Clark Expedition opened a whole new world to the Americans. It made everything seems possible. Most of all, it gave power to the idea that we were meant to expand West."

(Michael Witts, <u>Heading West: The Story of Lewis and Clark</u>, page 378)

Journal

A **journal** is a private notebook that is used for writing about anything you want. You can write about something interesting that happened to you, your ideas and feelings, or anything else that's on your mind.

Parts of a Journal

- The date at the top of each new entry
- A beginning that tells what the entry is about
- Important details that show your thoughts and feelings
- Informal language that sounds like you're talking to a friend

> **The date of the entry is at the top of the page.** → February 1

> **The beginning tells what the journal entry is about.** →

I hate it when people ask me what I want to be when I grow up. I mean, how am I supposed to know? I'm only in fourth grade! My mom says that when people ask me this question, they're really just trying to figure out stuff about me, like what I'm interested in. So, that got me thinking. I started thinking about all of the things I like, and how I might make one of them into a job.

> **Details explain your thoughts and feelings.** →

Well, I really like looking at the stars at night. Maybe it would be cool to be an astronaut. I bet the stars look pretty bright in space. It would also be fun to float around. I could do somersaults in the air and pretend like I'm swimming. I always wondered what's on the dark side of the

Other Journal Uses
Brainstorming
Problem Solving
Sketching
Story Writing
Writing Poems
Memories
Learning Log
Definitions

moon. I could probably find out if I was an astronaut. The only problem is that astronauts go really high in the air. I'm not a fan of heights.

It would be pretty awesome if I were a chef, though. After all, I love to eat. My dad makes the best green bean casserole. It actually looks kind of gross, but it's really good. And my mom makes a killer fruit salad with fresh lemon juice. But, here's the thing—I don't like to cook. It takes a lot of time to chop everything up. Doing the dishes and cleaning up afterward isn't fun, either. So, I guess being a chef isn't the job for me, either.

Maybe I should be a zookeeper. Animals are so cool! I love my dog, Butch, and my cat, Button. I don't even mind taking care of them. Well, I sort of don't mind. It's not very fun to clean the litter box. And Butch whines when I brush him. That makes me feel really bad for him. Besides, zookeepers have to take care of big animals. I'm not so sure that I would like doing that.

My cousin says I should join a circus. I know she's joking, but that could be pretty fun. I could learn to juggle and be a clown. Or maybe I could be one of those people who make lions jump through hoops. I also wouldn't mind learning the trapeze. It would be a blast to fly through the air like that. I probably wouldn't be scared of the heights because I would know that there's a net below to catch me. Then again, who am I kidding? Circuses travel everywhere. I like staying close to home.

Ugh! I'm right back where I started. I still don't have a clue about what I want to be when I grow up. I have figured out one thing, though. I wish that people would stop asking me what I want to be. Instead, they should ask me what I'm interested in. I sure know a lot about that!

Index